Epic of Gilgamesh

Epic of Gilgamesh

An Annotated Prose Rendition
Based upon the Original Sumerian, Akkadian,
Babylonian, and Hittite Tablets

With Supplementary Texts
of Related Sumerian Lore and Selected Sumerian
Proverbs

Originally Published: 2001
Revised: 2018

John D. Harris

Hungry Point Press
Wabasha • Minnesota

For my nephew, Michael

Table of Contents

Introduction

The *Epic of Gilgamesh* is the oldest written chronicle in the world, composed three to four thousand years before Christ. It tells events in the life of a king in an ancient city of Mesopotamia. The text is revered, and the hero is an icon of Mesopotamia, equal in tradition to the Jewish hero David as told in the Bible or the Greek hero Achilles as told in the *Iliad*, both of which it precedes as literature and in some aspects it anticipates. For untold centuries, even into the last millennium before Christ, the children of what is now Iraq learned to read and write by copying *Gilgamesh*, just as once Greek children learned to read and write by copying the *Iliad* and just as before the 20th century in Europe and America children learned to read and write from the text of the Bible. References to Gilgamesh in daily speech were commonplace. To dig a well was to dig Gilgamesh's well. Certain rituals were referenced to his legend. Various walls or monumental buildings were referred to Gilgamesh's reign for almost two thousand years.

The legends of Gilgamesh were probably told at the earliest moment of that civilization called Sumerian, about 3500 BC, or more than 5500 years ago. Sumer was the first civilization, so-called, because historically here is the earliest known development of large city-states and written language.[1] In Egypt, China and Meso-America civilization would also independently develop. However, it is the Sumerian that is the immediate and profound

---

[1] Defining civilization is a topic for a book. However, these two characteristics—the city-state system and a written language capable of narration—are practically agreed upon by scholars. These developments poised the larger creation of imperial states that were to come: well-ordered administration of communications and commerce necessary for an economic and political commonwealth that would encompass hundreds and thousands of square miles and hundreds of thousands of people with many ethnicities.

progenitor of our own tradition. Elements of Sumer remain with us: in astronomy (our zodiac); in the manner that we tell time (the twelve hours on our clock) and in our calendar (the twelve months of the year); in some commonplace words such as sugar; and more subtly in the pattern of our lives and beliefs. We are and have been continuously, for example, a society of oligarchy, whose hierarchy and heritage is a military and economic dominance. We are a society of classes, defined by economic means, occupations and genealogy. We are a society of multi-cultural diversity that is tense with conflicted values, in which a more or less majority population is able to dominate language, legal and cultural affairs. And our institutions of governance, religion and commerce retain a recognizable continuity and similar function to that of this ancient civilization over a span of more than five thousand years.

The river plains around and between the Tigris and Euphrates rivers (hence, the term "Mesopotamia" or "between rivers" from the Greek) were populated from the coast of the Arabian sea (into which the rivers flowed), to the Zagros Mountains that border the plains to its east, and to far north and west, beyond the source of the rivers, where mountains separate these plains from the Mediterranean basin. The peoples of this broad land had a diverse ethnicity: Sumerian, Semite, Indo-European, and other native and foreign groups in lesser numbers.[2] Certain tensions between these various societies developed: between the city dweller and the rural;

---

[2] The Sumerian people are obscure; their language with its monosyllabic words is not related to any other that we know. The Semites carried cultural and linguistic traditions that can be traced to the Arab and the Jew today, and in the ancient world were related to the Assyrian, Babylonian, Aramaic (Palestinian), even Egyptian. Among the outsiders are those so-called Indo-Europeans who migrated from the steppes of Asia in waves over a long period (roughly 4500-2000 BC) to become the hosts of Europe and England (Germanic, Celtic, Latin, and so on), and also the Greeks, the Persians and the Aryans of India—to name the most well-known.

between the farming populations and the nomadic herdsmen; between the people of the cultivated plains and the people of the "open country." In its earliest development this was a distinction between the Sumerian people and the Semites who lived largely as nomadic herdsmen, like the Jews, as they are described in the Bible; the vilification of cities and city life in the Bible exemplifies these cultural prejudices very well.[3] Many Semitic peoples adapted to the "city life," taking to villages in the suburbs of the city, providing livestock to feed the city, and many were assimilated into the city. Within a thousand years, Semitic names outnumber Sumerian in the texts. Gradually the political and religious leadership shifted from Sumerian to the Semitic, until finally by 1800 BC or so, there were no more Sumerian rulers and the language of Sumer was dead, unspoken, but kept for sacred text and royal communications, much like Latin was kept by the Europeans long after the Roman Empire ceased to exist.

The complete text of the *Epic of Gilgamesh* did not fully survive in Sumerian, but only in the Semitic language of Akkadian. This collection of clay tablets—twelve in all—comes from the last period of the Akkadian Empire (circa. 700 BC), buried in the rubble of Nineveh when the Persians destroyed that city in 612 BC and discarded the old religion that had held sway for so long and began a new cultural tradition. The legend of Gilgamesh now disappeared.

---

[3] The classic citation is Genesis Chapters 18-19 where Sodom and Gomorrah are destroyed for their wickedness: ".... He overthrew those cities and all the plain, and all the inhabitants of the city, and that which grew upon the ground." Prophets of later times invoked this judgment—Isaiah, Jeremiah, Ezekiel—not only against heathen cities, but even against Jerusalem, wherever backsliding Jews had taken up the culture and especially the religious customs (idolatry) of city life.

Certain motifs and specific lore that first appeared in the *Epic of Gilgamesh* did persist after it had completely disappeared by name. You will recognize the story of the Flood, which became a part of Hebrew lore, retold as the tale of Noah, but also retold in Greek mythology. You may also recognize other elements that remind you of other ancient myths: the descent to the underworld where the dead dwell, the struggle with monsters, the pursuit of immortality. Some scholars have noted specific parallels to Homer's *Odyssey*: the offense to the gods for slaying the sacred cattle of the sun, the sojourn of the hero with a woman who guides him on his quest. But the name of Gilgamesh was forgotten when these other tales were told, forgotten with the language that had uttered it, and his name would have remained unspoken forever but for the archeology that recovered it some two thousand years later.

After Nineveh was destroyed and sacked, it was never again occupied, a forbidden place, and over the ages it was scavenged, and its ruins weathered, but local legend still preserved its identity. In 1839 a young British officer, traveling between military assignments, chanced upon that local legend; he was wealthy enough to engage labor at his own expense and so began an excavation. He found the site of the royal library and in its buried chambers, tens-of-thousands of clay tablets in a strange language. For over a decade after the tablets had been rescued and shipped off to the British Museum, their words could not be successfully translated, until a rock inscription was found that contained a key to its strange cuneiform characters (the so-called Record of Darius). Then in 1872, after sorting through many thousands of tablets, most of which were mundane records of royal administration and accounting, the *Epic of Gilgamesh* was recognized. With it—and most exciting at the time—was the discovery of an ancient tale of the "biblical" Flood, predating the Bible itself. Just one year before, Darwin's theory of the descent of man had been published, scandalizing England, and so for some

4

this discovery was now another heretical challenge to the presumptive history of mankind as reckoned by the Bible. To others, however, the discovery affirmed the truth of the Bible.[4]

The *Epic of Gilgamesh* is called an "epic" in the tradition of the Greek *Iliad* or the medieval *Beowulf* only because of certain outward similarities: like these, it is a chronicle of a cultural hero; like these, the events represent deeply meaningful, frequently recited subjects. Unlike these other epics, the *Epic of Gilgamesh* was not known to be recited to music as entertainment by bards. In its native text it seems not composed as song at all.[5] Still, it was written down, we are told, to be read aloud on some occasion, although probably not in association with any particular religious occasion; it was serious secular entertainment.

Like epic poems, the central figure is admired for his prowess and power; he is a heroic warrior, whose greatest adventure is here recounted. Like these epics, this text is also characterized by its repeated formulaic epithets and catch-lines, and an aesthetic for repetition generally, as if its passages were composed for memorization and recitation. Thus, it resembles the cadence, style and structure that classically arise in the same sort of oral traditions that created the Greek and Old English epic poems. In short, the *Epic of Gilgamesh* shows all the characteristic features of a mythic lore that must have been told and retold over the ages, as the sacred memory of a people. It resembles in this way all mythic lore; that

---

[4] George Smith, an assistant in the British Museum, made the discovery. On reading the text he "... jumped up and rushed about the room in a great state of excitement, and, to the astonishment of those present, began to undress himself."

[5] Some scholars insist the Epic is "poetic" and that in pointed parts it might have been intentionally written as a poem. But we do not evidence of rhyme schemes *per se* or a specific measured meter. That being said, the writing is artful and contains structural qualities that are like a formal poem. See Background: Translation of the Text for a fuller discussion of the issue.

also of Native Americans, of African tribes, and of aboriginals all over the world, possessing a style in story telling that seems similar, having subject matters that are fantastic and ultimately magical, intentionally going beyond the normal bounds of the world.

Gilgamesh, in this sense, belongs to the tradition of all mythical heroes whose adventures take place in a reality that transcends us or that in another sense is always present. It is the realm of eternity. It is the "other world" where what is human is strange, what is human lacks normal power or significance. Literatures like this, motifs like these, predominate ancient and primitive literature, what is customarily called mythology. The dream-like quality, a deliquescence of thought, wherein reality and state of mind liquidly exchange and what is real is symbolic, and what is symbolic becomes what is real: this state of magic is natural to these tales. It is the essence of their wisdom, for they are speaking from a mind that is entranced with what psychologists call the unconscious, those thoughts and experiences that are instinctive or elemental or profoundly personal.

This "mythic" manner of thinking and speaking is not only unfashionable—except when self-consciously fantastic; it is no longer believable. There are two schools of thought about the question of whether such tales were ever truly believed: one is that no one ever believed these myths, they were always recognized as metaphor or allegory; the other (in various forms) is that people did believe them but could not help themselves because they were "primitive" or they were intellectually inferior or their brains were different than ours. Of course, people still do believe in the "literal truth" of their sacred books. What makes the *Epic of Gilgamesh* less believable than, say, the Bible or the Koran or the Upanishads, is only that no one is still alive who does believe it. "The religions that we call false were once true," as Emerson said.

6

The *Epic of Gilgamesh* is an accidental artifact of a lost civilization that was submerged, covered over by intervals of history, surviving half-buried in hardly recognizable ruins and only doubtfully recalled by ancient enemies and foreigners who knew them mostly by legend. Yet, this was the first civilization, that which is the father and mother of our own civilization. It is like the great-great-great-grandparent whose name you do not know but without whom you would not exist. In that sense, when we read the *Epic of Gilgamesh* we are reading the recollections of our most ancient parents, their intimate moments, their fears and hopes and ambitions, when their body was vital, their mind keen, their heart speaking.

The language may sometimes seem stiff and formalistic. Some behavior is couched in customs or actualities that are not understood and are not explained. There are matters that are not believable to us—monsters, deities, and places that we do not think exist, nor ever existed. Yet, we can perceive in Gilgamesh a person like ourselves. We understand him, even if we do not understand or believe all that he does. Gilgamesh is the first of literature that expresses the human experience, if not a human individual. It is central to the legend that we believe he really lived. This is not the tale of a god. This is the tale of a man.

A Brief Word on This Rendition

As explained more completely in the appendix, this rendition of the *Epic of Gilgamesh* is based upon the literal translations of original tablets. These translations are given word-for-word and line-for-line, corresponding to specific tablets and columns. Because the many scholarly translators have so diligently reproduced the authentic text, they reveal gaps, questionable words, and confusing expressions that are found in the often-damaged tablets. These problems make those literal translations difficult and unrewarding for a casual reader or a student. This rendition seeks to fill the gaps as faithfully as possible with likely text and to clarify expressions and confusions with terms that are based upon an understanding of the ancient culture.

I have annotated the text to help readers with the names of gods and goddesses, customs and terms that they may not be familiar with. Footnotes further explain matters of the text, and citations at the margin correlate my rendition to the specific clay tablet in which the original text may be found. For reasons of story-telling, I have divided the tablets into a "prologue", followed by "adventures", and in one instance I have rearranged the traditional order.

A Comment on the Second Edition

This is the second published addition. In addition to "grace" of editing, I have added the several appendices, including narration of the death of Gilgamesh and the myth of his father Lugalbanda, whose own divine intervention is suggestively similar to that of his son. I have also incorporated other additional fragments to the text, as they are frequently found, including a remarkable find which suggests that the forests of Cedar Felling were animated by monkeys in the trees.

Prologue

Ishtar is the goddess of fertility and war, related by tradition to a lineage of such goddesses that ultimately include Astarte (Phoenician), Aphrodite (Cypriot and Greek) and Venus (Latin). They were recognized to be the same deity by the ancients themselves, although in the ancient concept their particularity was also held to be true.

Tablet I: Column 1

I shall tell the world about the man who found out all things, he who experienced everything, he who searched everywhere, and gained complete wisdom. He found out what was secret and uncovered what was hidden. He brought back the tale of times before the Flood. He journeyed far and wide, until weary and at last resigned. All these deeds are witnessed on the monuments of stone that he himself engraved.

It was he who built up the wall of Uruk, which shines like a copper band, surrounding the holiest shrine, Sheepfold of Eanna,[6] House of the Sky, the home of Ishtar. Look along the long line of its high battlements—no one will ever match them. Come up to its gateway that has stood since before anyone can remember. Look at the wall he built; these are baked bricks;[7] it is so well built only the first

---

[6] Eanna means "House of the Sky." It was the supreme temple of Uruk and the most sacred temple in all of Sumer. Built as a ziggurat or stepped pyramid, Herodotus reports that at the top of it was a shrine. During the festival of the New Year, a young unmarried girl gave herself to the god Anu (Marduk in the Babylonian period) who visited her during the night. By other testimony that god was the king or some other person who served as surrogate for the god in symbolic coitus.

[7] Baked bricks were the most expensive but also the most durable. In the southern plain of Mesopotamia, fuel for fire was hard to come by because of

men, the Seven Councilors who taught us all our skills, could have laid this foundation.

Inside this wall there lies one quarter that is city, one quarter that is orchards, one quarter that is clay pits, and then the open ground for Ishtar and her temple. These four parts: that is the city of Uruk.

Approach the temple Eanna, the home of Ishtar, which none can build more beautifully, dazzling with its mosaic walls of many colors.

Pass between the jeweled lions at her high doorway. Inside the temple now. Look for the copper cabinet. Undo its bronze lock. Draw open the doors to show the secret tablets, tablets of sky-blue lapis lazuli and read: this is the story of Gilgamesh who suffered so much.

He was a better king than all the others of his day, a warrior, powerful—a raging wild bull. He was a hero to the people of his city, Uruk. He marched at the front of them as their leader, or stood behind as their protector, a brother to all men, a net for them all. The flood-waves that overwhelm the walls could not overwhelm him.[8]

---

deforestation from so many centuries of a ravaging civilization, and so bricks were usually not fired.

[8] In fact, the walls of these cities were intended to ward off the flood as much as human enemies. They did not always protect the population from either.

Tablet I: Column 2

Son of Lugalbanda, one-time leader of Uruk, and son of Ninsun, the goddess, goddess of the Wild Cow, cow of the lofty sky: he is Gilgamesh, splendid and strong. He was the one who opened up the passes through the mountains when we were afraid to go there. He was the one who dug the canals across the plains even to the mountains. He crossed the ocean as far as the sunrise. He found the edge of the world, seeking an undying life, and reached the place beyond the world where lives Ut-napishtim, the man who does not die, he who restored the shrines and temples after the Flood ruined the cities.

The imperfect divinity of Gilgamesh is a characteristic of mythic heroes. In his case, it may also reference his birth by a woman serving surrogate to the goddess at her Temple.

Who can say "I am king," but Gilgamesh?
No one can compare to him.
Two-thirds divine, and one-third mortal.

[Lines damaged to end of this section]

11

The Adventure of Enkidu

In Uruk, the Sheepfold, he was the shepherd of his people, but he would walk about, proud, like a wild bull, his head held high, showing his superiority to all of us. He was overbearing. Day and night. He would raise his weapons even against his comrades.

He would not leave the young men alone, challenging them to the sport of *pukku*[9] and beating them. He had no rival. He had no challenger. He would not leave the young girls alone, even the daughters of warriors, even the young brides. The gods often heard their complaints. The young men became dejected, alone in their private quarters.

To the gods of heaven, to the lord of Uruk, they complained: "Did Aruru create such a rampant wild bull? Is there no rival? He is overbearing. Day and night. He is the shepherd of Uruk and yet he will not leave the young girls alone, even the daughters of the warriors, even the young brides. He will not leave the

Aruru is one of many names for the Mother Goddess. The many names are sometimes poetic epithets, but sometimes are wholly different entities, related to the many traditions or cultures and languages in which she was named. Customarily, ancient societies recognized and respected these variant names and often adopted and exchanged elements of worship, although in other respects they did not tolerate each other.

---

[9] In Dalley's notes *pukku* and *mekkû* are described to be respectively a stick and a hoop, instruments of a kind of field hockey. The game was evidently also

Anu is the sky god. The marriage of sky and earth as seminal creation of the world is the common conception in the religious tradition that becomes our heritage.

Ninurta is one of the next generation of gods, son of Ellil whose is "Lord of Men." He is called the champion or "avenger" of Ellil and is associated with war. Ninurta's main shrine was in the city of Nippur and was perhaps originally a tribal god.

young men alone. He raises his weapons even against his comrades."

They called especially upon Aruru: "You, Aruru, you created mankind. Now create someone to rival him, someone to bring peace to Uruk."

When Aruru heard this, she created inside of herself the word of Anu. Aruru washed her hands, pinched off a piece of clay, shaped it and cast it out into the open country. She created Enkidu, whose name means "wild man," offspring of silence, Sky-bolt of Ninurta who protects our herds, gives us our bread, leads us into battle. Like him, Enkidu is the Axe of war.[10]

His whole body was shaggy with hair, and he had tresses like a woman. His locks grew luxuriant and thick as grain. He knew nothing of people or life among them. He was naked as the animals. He ate with

---

associated with fertility rituals of Ishtar. Heidel cites other authorities that suggest these are instead a drumstick and drum. Given textual context, here and elsewhere — see Adventure of the Halub Tree (Tablet XII) — and the more recent scholarship, I prefer Dalley's interpretation.

[10] The three epithets for Enkidu—in Akkadian the *Word* of Anu; the *Axe* and the *Sky-bolt*—are also terms for specific attendants to the temple of Ishtar whose city Gilgamesh is disturbing. The usage here, if a conscious literary device, suggests that Enkidu is perceived as an agent of that religious order. The tension between the political warrior class and the caste of priests is inferred. They rivaled one another in wealth, authority and land. Gilgamesh was acting lawlessly. He could not be controlled, even by the moral authority of the priesthood, without a champion who equaled or exceeded the measure of his physical strength.

them. Like the gazelle he grazed. He crouches with the cattle to quench his thirst at pools. Living with the wild beasts, he is satisfied.

One day a thieving and murderous outcast who lived far from other men, who survived by hunting for his food, came face to face with Enkidu beside this watering place, as he was setting traps for his fare. He saw him again on three successive days. The hunter looked at him, dumbstruck. In perplexity he went to his wattle hut and stayed, mute and afraid. He worried and would not leave his hut. His face grew gaunt with fatigue, like that of a man who has traveled too far from home and is exhausted and haunted by grief.

Tablet I:
Column 3
His father came to visit him, and he made his voice to be heard and spoke:

"Father, there is a man who came from the mountain. He is strong. He is wild. He is like the Sky-bolt of Anu. He walks about the mountain like a wild beast. He eats with the cattle there. He waters with them. He stood in the water among them and saw me; and I am afraid to go there. He fills the pits that I dig for traps. He pulls out the snares that I have set. He helps the cattle, the other wild animals that I catch; he sets them free. He will not let me hunt."

His father told him to travel to Uruk, to seek Gilgamesh to help him.
[Lines damaged]

The hunter went off to see Gilgamesh. He took the road, set his face toward Uruk and came then to the presence of Gilgamesh who listened to what he had to say:

"There is a man who came from the mountain. He is strong. He is wild. He is like the Sky-bolt of Anu. He walks about the mountain

15

Shamhat (also spelled
"Shamkat" in the
Babylonian or
Shambat in the
Sumerian) is a word
meaning "voluptuous
woman" or also
"harlot", but it is used
here as a personal
name. The harlots of
Ishtar performed
sacred service for the
temple and were
institutional servants
as much as the various
functionaries of
priesthood; their
prostitution earned
wealth for the temple
and they themselves
often married well
after their term of
service. Their service
was also ritualistic;
annually at least there
was an enactment of
sacred sexual union for
the benefit of fertility
and the New Year.

Tablet I:
Column 4

like a wild beast. He eats with the cattle
there. He waters with them. He stood in
the water among them and saw me; and I
am afraid to go there. He fills the pits that
I dig for traps. He pulls out the snares that
I have set. He helps the cattle, the other
wild animals that I catch; he sets them
free. He will not let me hunt."

Gilgamesh replied:

"Go back, hunter, and lead the woman
Shamhat, who is harlot for our temple of
Ishtar, to that place. When he comes with
the cattle at the watering place she must
approach him and take off her clothes and
reveal her attractions to him. He will see
her and come close to her. Then the cattle
that have grown up with him in the open
country will become alien to him."

The hunter went; he led forth the harlot
Shamhat with him, and they took the road,
they made the journey to that place. In
three days, they reached that place. The
hunter and harlot hid and waited. One day
passed. Then a second day.

Then on the third day the cattle arrived at
the water and drank. And Enkidu, who
came from the mountain with them, who
shares their food and drinks with them at
the watering place, took his drink with

16

them also. Shamhat saw this wild man. The hunter, wicked outcast that he was, urged her now:

"Here he is now, Shamhat, show him your breasts. Spread open your legs for him. Let him see your attractions. Do not pull away but let him look. He will see you and come close to you. Drop your garments for him and let him lie down upon you. Do for him, the wild man, as women do for men. Then his cattle, which have grown up with him in open country, will become alien to him.

Shamhat took off her clothing and showed herself to Enkidu. She parted her legs and did not pull away from him. He lay upon her and she did for him, a wild man, as women do for men.

For six days and seven nights Enkidu was aroused and poured himself into Shamhat. When he was sated with her, he left her and set himself back to the open country. He came upon the gazelles but when they saw him, they scattered. All the cattle of the open country kept away from him now. For Enkidu had bathed with the woman, his body was too clean. Enkidu could not run with them as he had before; his legs now lacked the power; Shamhat had diminished him.

He had acquired knowledge of himself. It made him different.

He went back to the watering place and sat at the harlot's feet. The harlot studied his face. He listened carefully to what she told him:

"You have become profound, Enkidu, you have become like a god. Why should you roam the open country with the wild animals? Let me take you to Uruk, the Sheepfold of Eanna, to that pure House of the Sky, the home of Anu and Ishtar, where Gilgamesh rules, stronger than any man, who is like a wild bull."

Enkidu heard and agreed, knowing it true in his own
mind:

"Take me, Shamhat. Take me to the House of the Sky, home of
Anu. Take me to Gilgamesh who is stronger than any man, who is
a wild bull. I will go to Uruk. In Uruk, I shall be the strongest. I
shall go and alter destiny. For one who is born in the open country
is strongest."

Shamhat answered:

"Come, Enkidu, and go with me to Uruk, where the young men
gird their waists with sashes, where every day is a feast day, where
the drums beat and the girls show themselves, adorned only in joy
and full of happiness. In bed at night, the great men enjoy
themselves, Enkidu.

"Let me tell you about Gilgamesh, a man of joy and woe at once.
Look at him. Observe his face. He is beautiful in his manhood,
dignified. His body is seductive to women. He is powerful,
stronger than you. He does not sleep. Night or day. O Enkidu,
change your mind for punishing him. Shamash, the Sun, loves
Gilgamesh. And Anu (the Sky), and Ellil (father of the Gods), and
Ea (the Earth) made him wise.

"Before you came from the mountains, Gilgamesh dreamt of you.
He arose and described his dream, he told it to his mother.

> 'Mother,' he said, 'I saw a dream in the night.
> There were stars in the sky for me and a sky bolt
> fell upon me. It crushed me. I tried to lift it off, I
> tried to move it aside, but it was too heavy. The
> people, the men of Uruk were standing by, and

18

had gathered around. The men crowded about it.
The young men were attracted to it. They kissed
it like young children would. Then I myself
loved it. As if it were a wife. I doted on it. I
brought it to you, and you yourself treated it as a
son, a brother to me.'

Tablet I:
Column
6 "His mother, the wise Wild Cow, Ninsun, all-knowing,
understood and spoke:

'When there were stars in the sky for you, and
something like a sky-bolt kept falling upon you,
you tried to lift it up, you tried to turn it over,
but you could not budge it. You carried it to me,
laid it at my feet; I treated it as equal to you.
And you loved it as a wife and doted on it. It
means a strong partner shall come to you, one
who can save the life of a friend. He will be the
most powerful in strength in all the lands. His
strength will be as great as the sky-bolt. You
will love him as a wife; you will dote on him.
And he will always keep you safe. That is the
meaning of your dream.'

"Gilgamesh spoke to his mother and told her:

'Mother, I have had a second dream. An axe
was thrown down in the street. The men
crowded about it. The young men were
attracted to it. They kissed it like young
children would. Then I myself loved it. As if it
was a wife. I doted on it. I brought it to you,
and you yourself treated it as a son, a brother to
me.

"His mother, the wise Wild Cow, Ninsun, all-knowing, understood and spoke:

'The copper axe that you saw is a man. You will love it as a wife and dote on it. A strong partner shall come to you, one who can save the life of a friend. He will be the most powerful in strength in all the lands. His strength will be as great as the sky-bolt.'

"Gilgamesh spoke to his mother: Let it fall, then, according to the word of Ellil, the great counselor. I shall gain a friend."

Thus Shamhat had heard of the dreams of Gilgamesh and told them to Enkidu.

Tablet II:
Column 1

She told him: "The dreams mean that you will love one another."

[The entire text is impossible to read]

Tablet II:
Column 2

[The text of this section is heavily damaged]

See
Babylonian
Tablet II:
Column 2

Shamhat shared her clothing with Enkidu; one garment she wore and the other he wore. She took his hand, and like a mother, she led him away. She led him to a village of shepherds nearby where the people were amazed to see him: "He is like Gilgamesh himself, strong and manly. He is as powerful in his arms as a sky-bolt of Anu."

He entered the hut of a shepherd.

They brought him food and drink but he would not take it, not understanding it.

Babylonian Tablet II: Column 3

He is used to the suck of milk from the teats of wild cattle, not beer. He stared. Enkidu knew nothing of eating bread or drinking beer. He had never learned. Shamhat made her voice heard and spoke to Enkidu: "Eat the bread, Enkidu, it is sacred to life. Drink the beer; it is the Providence of our fertile land."[11]

Enkidu ate the bread until he had enough. He drank the beer, seven whole jars, and he felt joyful and comfortable. His heart rejoiced. His face beamed. He anointed his body as any man does and put on the clothes of a man. He took up a weapon and now was like any warrior.

He stayed with these sheepherders. He fought the lions and drove them off. He slew wolves that harassed their flocks. So the herdsmen could sleep at night while Enkidu guarded.

[The text is damaged]

Babylonian Tablet II: Column 4

One day a young man hurried through the village and Enkidu stopped him. Shamhat approached him to ask him: "Where are you going?

---

[11] Sandars invokes the Biblical phrase here, calling bread the "staff of life" and turns the beer into wine. That might make readers think there was a literary parallel to the Bible that there is not. I prefer Dalley's literal translation that bread is "the symbol of life" and beer is "the destiny of the land." But these do not perhaps convey the emotional significance of the phrases, so I have rendered them as you see.

The man explained: "I hurry to the assembly of the father's-in-law where I am to fill the table of ceremonies with delightful food. They shall bring forth the brides for the bridegrooms, chosen for them, as is the custom and the Providence of the land.

But Gilgamesh, the king of Uruk, usurps them. He claims by right of his birth, by a prophecy made when his umbilical was cut, that he may take each bride to bed before her husband shall and forces himself upon them. They cannot stop him.

He takes the brides and will not give them back, even to their mothers." [12]

[The text is damaged]

---

[12] It would appear the custom to organize weddings on the occasion of a certain time of the year, possibly also associated with ritual or a sacred day; or perhaps simply a practical matter, an occasion when people may gather and the expense of feasting may be a shared burden. Such exchange of brides and bridegrooms at periodic gatherings is common among nomadic peoples, such as herdsmen. At any rate, marriage was a family decision, and possibly a tribal decision, if the assembly here has any wider meaning. In Sandars' translation, which is not supported by the literal text but is plausible, the wedding is the sacred marriage of the New Year festival and the bride to be selected is that which would lie with the god Anu. By implication, Gilgamesh's usurpation may be some sacrilege.

Some scholars argue that this sexual usurpation of the husband is an act of *jus primae noctis* which most familiarly was the right of some medieval European kings to claim a bride upon her wedding night for himself, a profound assertion of dominance, but one that may also have a spiritual, if not animal, significance. For what child thence issues from such marriage may thus be his. It may be here (as elsewhere) that this kingly right was largely gestured more than practiced. So Gilgamesh had overstepped custom. But the text also adds that he takes the brides and will not surrender them afterwards, a true outrage.

Babylonian Tablet II: Column 5

Enkidu went in front and Shamhat behind him and they entered Uruk.

He stood in the street of Uruk, the Sheepfold, and the people gathered about him, and gaped at him. The men massed. The young men crowded about him. They kissed his feet like very young children. They spoke among themselves:

"He is just like Gilgamesh."

Some said he was shorter, but others said he looks very strong. Someone told how the mountains gave him birth where he grazed with wild cattle, how he sucked milk at the teat of the wild cow.

"We shall make sacrifices to give thanks for him, for he looks to be noble. A match is found for Gilgamesh at last."

Babylonian Tablet II: Column 6

The bed was made each night for a wedding, as was the custom, for the union of Ishhara[13] and each night Gilgamesh came and took the place of bridegroom to these brides.

But now Enkidu stood in the threshold of the marriage house and barred the way of Gilgamesh. Gilgamesh, enraged, enraged by his lust, confronted Enkidu.

Enkidu blocked his passage and would not let him enter. They grappled like wrestlers. They tossed their bodies against the doorway and the doorposts shattered. The walls shook. The walls crashed and the door fell. They fell into the street and wrestled.

---

[13] The "union of Ishhara" is a folk wedding ceremony. Having prepared the bed for the wedded couple with this spiritual intent, the conjugation reenacts the love of Ishtar and her consort.

Blending
Akkadian
Tablet II:
Column 4
&
Babylonian
Tablet II
Column 7
Enkidu at last threw Gilgamesh to the ground.[14]

Bitterly Gilgamesh wept and his mother Ninsun, goddess of the Wild Cow, listened and spoke to him, but Gilgamesh was inconsolable: "He is born in open country. He is wild. Who can better him?"

Gilgamesh rose and turned to walk away, but Enkidu who had stood watching, listening, sat down and began to cry.

Gilgamesh turned back.

Enkidu wept.

Gilgamesh embraced Enkidu and asked: "Why are your eyes full of tears?"

Enkidu told him: "Gilgamesh, your mother bore you to be unique. The Wild Cow of the Sheepfold, Ninsun; she gave you protection even from death. And Ellil who rules all decreed that you shall rule men."

---

[14] The text is completely ambiguous on this point. It may be that Enkidu was thrown down and so bested in the contest, or that Gilgamesh was thrown down. But the bitter weeping of Gilgamesh and the appearance of his mother, the goddess — very like the scene in the *Iliad* when Achilles loses face and is disconsolate, only to be comforted by his mother — suggests that it is Gilgamesh who was bested and so Enkidu's compassion, even more his admiration, restores Gilgamesh and they are made equals in each others eyes. For Enkidu is not destined to be a king, but a friend or servant of a king.

The reader should know that the customary interpretation is that Gilgamesh defeats Enkidu in wrestling, as it may have seemed unthinkable to early translators that any hero should be bested in combat and so that has become the common translation. But for the reasons cited it seems wrong to me.

24

After this day, they were inseparable friends. Gilgamesh loved him as if he was his wife. He doted on him. He took him to his mother and she treated him as an equal, as if Enkidu were her son and Gilgamesh was his brother.

The Adventure of the Forest of Cedars

[The text of this episode is much damaged in both the Akkadian and the Babylonian series; rather than indicating the frequent gaps and ambiguities, the text is reconstructed from the best sources, including the more ancient Sumerian.[15] Much is conjectural, and is given some poetic license. The Sumerian, rather than the Akkadian, contains more details, and so the temper of the story reflects its more "archaic" tone.]

Sumerian Tablets

Gilgamesh speaks to Enkidu: "In Uruk people are dying, people are suffering. I lean out over the city wall: bodies in the water almost make the river overflow. That is what I see: no one is tall to heaven; no one is large to the land; no one fights back the rising grasp of his own grave. I see this in my father and my mother. I see this by my own god Ea."[16]

"I want to go to the mountains of cedar-felling, to give my name renown, if I can. If I fail, I will give renown to the gods." Enkidu answered him: "My lord, if today you go to the mountains of cedar-felling, Shamash should be told. The mountains of cedar-felling belong to Shamash."

---

[15] During the invasion of Iraq by America in 2003, many artifacts of the ancient world were destroyed or dispersed in pillage. One partial Babylonian version of Tablet 5 emerged a few years later in the clandestine market of such treasures, adding some lines which had been missing. These have now been incorporated.
[16] The gods in Sumerian are Enki (for the later Ea, the god who created mankind), and Utu (for the sun-god Shamash as shown here). Significantly the signature gods are consistently referenced in the tales, although the names of them may vary over the length of millennia and the difference between cultures.

27

Gilgamesh made sacrifice; he clasped a white kid to himself; he held a sacred instrument and he spoke to Shamash: "Shamash, I am going into the mountains of cedar-felling. Help me to go."

From heaven Shamash replied to him: "Young man, you are already fortunate and well blessed. What would you want with the mountains?"

"Shamash, in Uruk people are dying, people are suffering. I lean out over the city wall: bodies in the water almost make the river overflow. That is what I see: no one is tall to heaven; no one is large to the land; no one fights back the rising grasp of his own grave.

"I want to go to the mountains of cedar-felling, to give my name renown, if I can. If I fail, I will give renown to the gods."

Tablet II: Column 5 & 6

Babylon Tablet III

Gilgamesh found Enkidu in distress, weeping as someone in mourning, shuddering as someone in terror. He looked tormented with some dread and his eyes were filled with tears. Gilgamesh lowered his face and said to Enkidu: "Why are your eyes filled with tears? Why are you so tormented?"

Enkidu made his voice heard and spoke to Gilgamesh:
"Howls of grief, my friend; grief agonizes me; my face distraught. My arms feel feeble, my body feels weak.

"I know this place you seek. I know this Humbaba you seek. Ellil has destined him to rule the cedar forests, to terrify those who enter

28

them. All those who enter them are seized with a sickness unto death; their life is slowly removed from them."

A line drawing of a terra-cotta mask, said to be the face of Humbaba, the creature of the Cedar Forest whom Gilgamesh and Enkidu should challenge for the felling of the trees. The title "god of the fortress of intestines" is given to him and his face is thought to be representation of coils of entrails.

Gilgamesh did not reply. Enkidu could not change his mind, but Enkidu continued:

"His voice is the rushing flood, his breath is
unearthly fire, and brings a burning-to-death. He
hears keenly all who come into his forest, he can
hear travelers who are on the edge of his forest, who

are yet twenty days away from him,[17] so who can approach him unawares?

"I know him, Gilgamesh. When I lived in the open country, when I went to the mountains with the other animals, I went into that dark forest. His voice was a rushing flood; his breath was pure fire. Why do you want this? Humbaba's home is impossible for us."

Gilgamesh made his voice heard and he spoke to Enkidu: "My friend, I want to go. You should come with me. We shall go to the forest of Humbaba, take our axes, and take from him his fragrant cedar for our roof beams and our doorposts and lintels. If we must, we shall kill Humbaba."

Enkidu made his voice heard and spoke to Gilgamesh: "How can we go to the cedar forest? Humbaba never sleeps. He is guardian to the forest. His seven terrors keep the forest protected from men."

Gilgamesh made his voice heard and spoke:

"Who can go up to heaven, my friend? Only gods dwell with Shamash forever.[18] Mankind can number his days. Whatever he achieves, it is only wind.[19] Are you afraid to die? Where is your courage?

---

[17] A single unit measurement of distance in the Akkadian is the equivalent of 2 hours of travel. Assuming that these heroes can travel for 12 hours in a day, it shall take twenty days to reach the center of the forest where Humbaba is found.

[18] According to Sumerian-Assyrian cosmogony, Shamash (the sun) travels to an outer sphere of the heavens after each day, and there the gods always enjoy the light and benefits of warmth and radiance.

[19] Compare to Ecclesiastes 1:14 "I have seen all the works that are done under the sun, and behold all is wind and vexation of the spirit."

"I will go in front of you, and your voice behind me will shout out: 'Don't be afraid. I am here.' If should die, I will have won fame. People will say: 'Gilgamesh fought ferocious Humbaba. He was born to be great.' But you, you grew up in the open country. When a lion sprang at you, you took him in combat. You have said so to me. It makes me jealous to think of it.

"Come, my friend, we will go and take down those cedars, and our fame will last forever. Let's go to the forge and cast those axes now."

They sat afterwards with their new weapons and admired them. They made double-headed axes, as warriors use, and narrow-headed axes as carpenters use. The warrior axe weighed one whole talent of bronze to each. The swords that were made for them weighed one whole talent of bronze to each. Their belts were fitted to hold them, and the sheaths for each sword weighed one whole talent of bronze each.

Gilgamesh and Enkidu went to the assembly of the young men to reassure them, for they had heard all over the city what Gilgamesh meant to do.

Gilgamesh spoke to the young men: "Listen to me, my comrades, you who know me as a fellow warrior, you know that I am adamant. I shall take the road to Humbaba. I shall face the unknown. I shall take the unknown path. Give me your blessing. It will be so. I will return in time, I will come to the City gate, and I will enter in time to celebrate the New Year festival and will take your oaths and give my own. Joy will resound. There will be shouts of joy ringing from Eanna, the House of the Sky."

The New Year's festival was set by the lunar calendar and the time of planting and was an occasion of renewal of the earth and the nation. Oaths were exchanged between the people and their king. Ceremonially the institutions of temple and kingship were unified. In Babylon at the temple of Ishtar the ceremony concluded with the sacred marriage as described by Herodotus.

Gilgamesh and Enkidu went to the assembly of the old men to reassure them, for they had heard about what Gilgamesh meant to do.

Enkidu spoke to the old men: "The young men of Uruk tell him not to go to the cedar forests where Humbaba lives and protects the forest. They tell him that this is a journey not to be undertaken."

The great counselors of Uruk stood up and gave their opinion to Gilgamesh: "You are still young, Gilgamesh, you are impetuous. You are brave, but you do not know what you will find there. Humbaba, whose voice is rushing flood, whose breath is deadly fire; he can hear men coming to him who are more than 20 days away. Whoever goes down into his forest is made sick unto death; the life in them is slowly taken away. Ellil destined him to keep the forests. Who, even among his own generation of gods, can face him?"

Tablet III: Column 1

Gilgamesh listened to the counselors and he reassured them: "You know me as your king; you know that I am adamant. I shall take the road to Humbaba. I shall face the unknown. I shall take the unknown path. Give me your blessing. I will return, I will come to the city gate, and I will enter in time to celebrate the New Year festival and will take your oaths and give my own. Joy will resound. There will be shouts of joy ringing from Eanna, the House of the Sky."

The Counselors replied: "Do not trust entirely in your own strength, Gilgamesh. Stalk him carefully. Take aim of him carefully. Make your first blow take him.

"Let Enkidu go in front of you as you travel. He who leads the way will save the comrade. He knows the forest. He will guard his friend. He can watch over the fight and instruct your combat. Let Enkidu guard his friend, keep his comrade safe.

"Let him bring his friend back to be the bridegroom of our goddess. So that we in our assembly may rely on our king and so that you as our king may rely on us."

Gilgamesh made his voice heard and spoke to Enkidu: "Come, my friend. We will go to the temple. To see Ninsun, our mother, who is wise, all-knowing, she understands these things. She will tell us what the Gods think of this."

They held hands as they walked and went to the temple.[20] The two went up the many-leveled staircases into the dwellings of the temple. They entered into her presence and Gilgamesh stood before her and spoke:

> "Ninsun, I am adamant. I will take the path across the distances to where Humbaba lives. I will face the unknown. I will take the unknown road. Until I have

---

[20] In Dalley's literal translation, they go to the palace and Ninsun is called queen. She is now no longer the divine presence, as Achilles mother was, but a person with whom Gilgamesh lives. Nevertheless, the context of the text suggests that it is not a "palace" but the temple of Ishtar in which she is to be found. This would be consistent with a rendering of Ninsun as priestess of Ishtar. Heidel's version specifically cites rites of a priestess, endowing Enkidu and Gilgamesh with holy protections.

reached that cedar forest. And if I must, I will kill Humbaba. I will purge from that place that Sickness unto Death, that Evil of the forest that Shamash hates."[21]

Tablet III:
Column 2

Ninsun listened carefully to her son and then entered her private chamber and bathed and prepared herself with ablutions and put on the ceremonial garment, the adornments, the twin-faced pins upon the breast and her headdress and went to the roof of the temple. She came before Shamash, made the smoke-offering, made a certain sacred offering prescribed for that, and raised her arms and asked: "Why have you given my son, Gilgamesh, a heart and mind so restless? Why do you choose him for this? You have influenced him and now he will take the distant path to where Humbaba lives. He faces the unknown. He will take the unknown road until he travels a long distance and comes to the Cedar Forest at last and then he will kill the ferocious Humbaba, and purge the forest of its demon, of that Sickness which you hate.

"Keep him, Shamash. Let Aya, your wife, the daughter-in-law, not be so afraid of you that she will not protect him. Trust the watchmen of the night to protect him."

Tablet III:
Column 4

Gilgamesh who had stood aside now extinguished the smoke sacrifice. He called to Enkidu and gave him his decision: "Enkidu, you are a strong man; although you are not of the same womb as I, you are my kin in

---

[21] Gilgamesh invokes a specific name of a demon that is associated with illness or misfortune. For consistency I associate it with the earlier description of the strange debilitating illness that overcomes persons who go deeply into Humbaba's forest.

strength. Your offspring will be dedicated to Shamash in remembrance of these oblations to Shamash. Priestess, devotee, and votaress: Shamash has placed this burden upon Enkidu. Enkidu will take a wife from the gods and will bring up daughters of the gods.[22]"

Ninsun addressed Enkidu: "Let Enkidu guard the friend. Let him keep his comrade safe. Let him bring him back safely for the brides of the New Year, so that our assembly may rely upon him again as king and he in turn may rely upon us."

But Enkidu was not persuaded and protested still to Gilgamesh: "My friend, turn away from this journey. I know this forest you seek. All those who enter them are seized with a sickness unto death; their life is slowly removed from them. I know this Humbaba you seek. I have seen him, Gilgamesh. His voice is a rushing flood; his breath is unearthly fire. Why do you want this?"

Babylonian Tablet III: Column 5

Gilgamesh replied, so disturbed by the reluctance of his friend that he had tears of emotion: "Enkidu, shall I live here, never to have made the journey my god calls me to make? Because I am afraid to die? Will I live forever in security anyway? Will I never die?

"I shall go, Enkidu. Shamash wants this of me. This will be done. I must be the one to do it.

"Go with me and bring me back safely, Enkidu. With Shamash, with you, I shall be protected."

---

[22] By this, we suppose he means that Enkidu will marry a priestess of Ishtar. As we may presume, it would be the woman Shamhat.

So the two prepared at last. Taking up the doubled-headed axes, each of which weighed one whole talent, and the axe of the builder to topple and hew the huge cedars, and the great bronze swords in their bronze sheaths, each of which weighed one whole talent.

At last, they went before the elders, the great counselors, and they were blessed by them, took advice from them for their journey.

"Make sure there is always water in your in waterskin," said one.

And another said: "Keep your eyes sharp and guard yourself well."

They reminded him to keep the god close to him: "Dig a pit when you stop for the night, make oblations to Shamash. You must libate cool water for Shamash. You must recall your father's name, too."

And they counseled him to keep Enkidu close to him: "Do not rely on your own strength, Gilgamesh. Let Enkidu walk ahead of you, to watch the paths and keep the road. He knows the entrances and ways of the forest and every trick of Humbaba. In the lead, he will keep his friend safe. He will guard you. And Shamash will let you win your combat.

And so they were blessed by the elders at last who said: "May your eyes gain the experience of your mouth's utterance. May he open up the closed path for you. May he prepare the way for your track. May he prepare the mountain for your feet. May he bring you the things that please you at night. May Lugalbanda, your father, stand beside you at your combat. Win as easily as children win. Afterwards may you wash your feet in the river of Humbaba."

The young men also wished them well and when they left the young men called after: "Go, Gilgamesh, and may your god go with you."

Tablet IV: Column 1   Enkidu and Gilgamesh traveled together. Side by side. They traveled a full day before they ate. They traveled well into the night before they took their rest. They did this day after day. The distance to the forest took them from the new moon to the full moon, and then three days more, and they came to the mountains of the north. Far beyond the fertile fields of Uruk, beyond the plains of the river, beyond ravine and ridge, as they came closer to the forest. The forest now stretched before them, wider than eye could see, higher than a great wall, dense with cedar in the thousands, and rising beyond the forest like the distant darkened heavens, the shaded mountains of Lebanon.

There they dug a pit for Shamash. They took water from the springs that came from the mountain and poured their libations of cool water, then refilled their water skins. They made an offering of flour to the Mountain. Gilgamesh prayed: "O Mountain, bring me a dream to help me."

Enkidu assisted his dreaming. He made Gilgamesh to rest and he made a circle of barley around him, he made a sacrifice with blood. Gilgamesh sat with his chin on his knees. Sleep, which spills over us, washed over him too. A dust devil appeared and Enkidu held it still.

In the middle of the night, at the time when the watch is changed at the gates, Gilgamesh started from his sleep. He stood up and said to his friend:

"My friend, did you speak to me? Why am I awake? Did you touch me? Why am I so upset? Did a god pass by? Why do I feel so weak?

Sumerian
Tablets "I had a dream, I know. And it is the dream that
upsets me. At the foot of the shaded mountain, in a
ravine, I looked up and the mountain fell over, on top
of us. We were helpless. We were like flies." [23]

Enkidu, who is born of the open country, helped his friend; he
explained his dream: "My friend, your dream is good. The
mountain you saw is this distant mountain. We will seize Humbaba
and kill him and leave his corpse to waste on the ground. At the
light of dawn we shall hear the word of Shamash, telling us this
dream is good."

After another whole day's journey, they ate their rations. They
came closer to the mountain, closer to the forest. When night came,
they took their rest. There they dug a pit for Shamash; as the
sunset, they dug the pit. Gilgamesh turned to the mountain and
made his flour offering: "O Mountain, bring me a dream to help
me."

Enkidu helped his dreaming. He made him rest and drew a circle
of barley about him. A dust devil came and Enkidu fixed it in
midair. Gilgamesh sat with his chin on his knees and sleep
overcame him, as it spills over all of us. In the middle of the night
he started. He stood up and said to Enkidu:

"Did you call me? Why I am awake? Did you touch me? Why am I
so upset? Did a God pass? Then why do I feel so weak?

---

[23] The Sumerian text is more complete for the adventure of the Pine Forest and
the slaying of Humbaba. To discriminate that text from the Akkadian, which this
retelling is otherwise based upon, I indicate by annotations where the text is
largely derived from Heidel's or Sandars' version of the Sumerian.

"I had another dream; it was the dream that upset me. Again, the mountain fell upon us as we passed beneath it and the rocks of it tangled my feet so I could not move. Then came an intolerable blazing light and inside that light some person who was inexpressibly beautiful; he pulled me out; he gave me water to drink and comforted me and then helped me to stand again."

Enkidu explained his dream: "Humbaba is like the mountain. He will fail as surely as the sun arises. We will stand over his body. I know that Shamash will favor us in the morning."

In one more day, they came to the gate of the forest of Humbaba, a gate built, they say, by the builders of Nippur, the holy city of Ellil, but no one knows why. It is wonderfully high, though not so high as the forest that looms beyond it. When they came upon the threshold of the gate, Humbaba knew they had come and they heard his voice, the rushing flood, the flood, which destroys cities, and like a raging bull, he crashed through the woods. Enkidu knew Humbaba must be near the gate and he wanted them to hurry and break it open and chase him, before Humbaba could gain the advantage. He raised his axe to break the seal of the gate, but he had not heart enough to destroy it, he admired it too much. But to his surprise, he only pushed on it and it flung open wide.

Gilgamesh now prepared to challenge Humbaba, to chase him into his forest lair, and Enkidu called back: "No, Gilgamesh, do not go into the forest. When I opened the gate, my hand lost its strength."

But Gilgamesh went ahead, past him, saying to his friend: "If we go together, we will protect one another. If we die, we will have fame."

They stood inside the gate. The sun was setting and shone golden light aslant the forest line; they stood in awe beside one another and gazed upon it, gazed and would not speak for a time. The forest shed a chill upon them, and enveloped them in its fragrance. Its presence was like a god. So huge. So lush. So vast.

Out of the forest as the light fell, as if by some intention, the noises of the animals therein arose. First the delicate evening calls of birds, intermittent and distinct. The mournful dove. The melodious thrush. The caw. The chit. Joining and increasing and compounding. Then the drone of insects like an enveloping undertone enlarged. Then the drubbing of frogs as a cadence to it all. And in the final telling voice, alarmed by human intruders, the mocking monkeys cried, who in the lofty branches swarmed in thrashing, unseen but for glints of their eyes and their ironic grins.

With darkness coming Gilgamesh dug the pit for Shamash and poured the libation of cool water and he did not forget to call his father's name. Turning toward the mountain, he poured the flour-offering and said again: "O Mountain, House of Heavens, bring me a dream to help me."

Tablet IV: Columns 3 -5   Again, and for the last time, Enkidu positioned Gilgamesh for his rest, drew the circle of barley about him and did other things to assist his dreaming. Gilgamesh sat with his chin on his knees and sleep overcame him like the waters. A dust devil appeared and Enkidu fixed it in midair. Then in the middle of the night, once more, Gilgamesh started, awakened suddenly and stood up and said:

"Did you call me? Why I am awake? Did you touch me? Why am I so upset? Did a God pass? Then why do I feel so weak?

"It was the dream, I know. It was the dream that came to me. The heavens roared and the earth roared up to the heavens. Daylight

40

failed. Darkness fell. Lightning flashed. Fire blazed out of the forest. Clouds gathered and ashes and coals rained down on us. Then the day reappeared and darkness disappeared and the fire was gone; only all was smoldering, all was ashen and charred all about us. I am afraid of this dream, Enkidu."

Enkidu had nothing to say. The sickness, the weakness that had enfeebled his hand seemed to overwhelm him. He looked at Gilgamesh without speaking.[24]

The two of them soberly watched till dawn and when the light made it possible, though all about them it was strangely silent, Gilgamesh decided he would take the trees as he had intended. He readied his axes. Enkidu readied his. With his ax sharpened and honed, Gilgamesh was the first to take down a tree at the edge of the forest, cleaving it so it would topple through the gateway.

When the tree fell, shattering branches, shuddering the ground, Humbaba heard it and felt the loss to his domain, like a part of him hurt, and wheeled to stalk Gilgamesh, advancing with increasing malice, increasing his speed.

---

[24] Interpretation of the third dream is absent from all tablets. Usually these dreams (and for that matter, many kinds of serial events) recur by the number three. It is a common convention, as you will recall from fairy tales you heard in childhood. But it seems that here the dramatic effect was to intentionally break the rule. The great remainder of the text is conjectural, taking suggestions from Heidel, Dalley and Sandars, as well as hints from fragmentary text. The order of the tablets and the episodes is so uncertain here, that I think the tradition was muddled, as it often is in oral traditions. Some episodes of the *Odyssey*, for example, are variations or addendum that various authors might omit or augment. Some legends of Penelope, for example, make her a faithless wife, who wantonly favored many men and, in the consequence, gave birth to a satyr: nothing could be more extremely different from the chaste Penelope of Homer's story.

Gilgamesh climbed atop the bole of the huge cedar and hacked the limbs, to sever them, to prepare the length of it for transport and carpentry.

Enkidu had not been able to help; he had not been able to stand. He told Gilgamesh now: "My friend, I cannot help you. I feel weaker still. Now I cannot lift this axe. I am frightened of this place."

Gilgamesh stopped his labor and went into the forest to search for certain plants; his mother had taught him where to look and what to seek, to find the plants, ones with succulent leaves that he would rub on Enkidu to relieve him, to stimulate and revive him. He went so deeply into the forest that he lost sight of Enkidu and the canopy of cedar shadowed the forest like dusk; no animals moved under it; the birds were high above the forest floor and could not be heard. The cedars, drizzling the sacred substance of their incense, showered him with the fine fragrant dew, sticky to touch.

He found out the paths of Humbaba and the tracks where he went to and fro; he crossed those paths warily and avoided them. Finally, when he had found the plants and had gathered enough, he turned back.

Something evil glided behind him.

Tablet IV: Column 6   Into the sun of afternoon he emerged and Enkidu was lying on the ground like an old man who wanted to die: "How can I go into the forest?"

Gilgamesh rebuked him: "Do not talk like a coward. We have come many days to be here. We have come to fell the trees for our household, you and me. You will not help me?"

He administered the plants to Enkidu's body. Enkidu too helped him, to rub the plants upon his limbs, his chest, to revive him.

Gilgamesh rose as Enkidu finished the medicine: "You have rubbed yourself with the plants, so you need not fear death. It has given double radiance to your body. Your shout will be like Humbaba. Like a kettledrum. The weakness will leave your hands and arms, and your legs will regain strength to stand and run. Take my hand, my friend. It is time we go into the forest. My heart burns for the contest. Forget death. Think only of life."

Enkidu stood and felt himself refreshed like a lion whose blood lust, whose fresh taste of mortal wounds has excited it, is invigorated, keen and alert. Gilgamesh said: "Now we are both ready to fight. You will go in front to guard your friend. It is said: the lion cannot defeat two of his cubs at once, and the twin-twined rope when bound together is the strongest rope. One alone cannot prevail."

Tablet V: Column 1 They stood together, each took up his weapons, an axe and the belted swords, and side by side, facing the forest, each of them silently considered his destiny. The forest stood silently before them. Within the forest, Humbaba silently watched them.

They stood before the path along which Humbaba went to and fro in the darkness of the forest. The mountain rose beyond, as the sun began now to decline in its daily track of the heavens. The shaded dwellings showed in its hiding features, dwellings of gods, shrines for Ishtar, where she is called Irnini, as she changes herself to that one here. The cedars spread serpentine into the ravines, luxuriant, and embrangled with fern and other undergrowth.

From the forest Humbaba's voice quietly rose up, like the surrounding sound of river rushing, it rose up and surrounded them: he said: "You are a fool, Gilgamesh, you and the brute animal you bring with you. Why do you come here? Your friend is still weak; and he is unworthy of you; he does not know his father's name, like the bastard of a beggar. You are both so small; you are no more to me than little turtles that do not even suck their mother's milk, so I would not want to touch you. Even if I were to kill you, eating you would not satisfy me." [25]

Gilgamesh did not speak. Enkidu did not speak. Humbaba's hidden eyes glowered. The malice that he felt was bitter as vomit in his mouth: "Gilgamesh, I will bite you through your windpipe and leave you to bleed, for the birds to devour your eyes and guts, and for other scavengers to eat your flesh."

Now Gilgamesh retreated, backwards, to the outside of the gate and Enkidu, guarding him, went backwards with him. Humbaba vented his breath through his nostrils, and fronds and branches of the cedar shriveled, as it passed through them, and reached the two who felt it like a bon fire.

Gilgamesh trembled now: "My friend, Humbaba is more terrible than I knew. He will leap on us and kill us before we can raise our

---

[25] The appearance of Humbaba is ambiguous. The Sumerian text reminds you of the various images of the dragon, a creature that is lion and serpent at once with the cunning of an evil man. Graphic representations of Humbaba are found in clay masks that may have been worn in ritualistic reenactments, showing a horrible face like an oriental demon, described by one scholar as a face of "coiled intestines." In one cylindrical seal, Humbaba has the figure of a man, apparently wearing such a mask. In the Akkadian and Babylonian text his description is vague and mysterious: the creature is formless and haunting, but possesses unearthly powers. In this way, Humbaba reminds me of the Tiamat myth, that primordial creature of chaos, which the ancient heroic god must conquer for the world to emerge.

44

swords. Did you feel his breath? It was like the forge of the coppersmith."

Enkidu replied to him calmly: "You are feeling the sickness of the forest that I felt. We cannot hide here. We cannot turn back."

Gilgamesh turned toward the sun, to Shamash; terrified, he looked for courage: "Remember what you said in Uruk? Do you hear me?" Through his tears his vision was blurred.

A voice came down to him from out of the sky: "Gilgamesh, child of Uruk, King of Earth, do not let him go deeply into the woods. He is not yet clothed in all his seven cloaks, those seven terrors by which he destroys men. He appears now only in this one. He terrifies you now only with his voice."

Tablet V:
Column 2

(Tablets of Nineveh are combined with those of Uruk to make a complete text)

So, Gilgamesh and Enkidu drew out their swords, as the sun set, and the forest gleamed with its light. Humbaba withdrew in stealth. Their swords showed streaks of verdigris, new and unused as they were. But these were not new and unused warriors.

They took to the path together, going into the forest. They took to the track of Humbaba. They pursued him into the darkness, swiftly now before the sun failed them.

Humbaba called back to them: "Why do you not go?"

Enkidu answered: "The lion cannot defeat two of his cubs at once, and the twin twined rope when bound together is the strongest rope."

They pressed Humbaba into the depths of the forest. Or did Humbaba draw them deeper into his realm? For the sun now was almost below the horizon and in the shadow of the trees it was already like night. Against the wall of the mountain they came, towering over them with the face of the rock, rising high above the forest to where the final glow of failing light showed like flame, and beyond it midnight sky. It was like a dream to them. Humbaba was gone. He had escaped.

Or were they trapped now in the darkness of the forest at the edge of night?

Again the forest surging sang. Again the birds in cacophony and the insects throbbing. The monkeys screaming and wildly dashing.

What is Humbaba? What animal? What god? Whose voice was a weapon like the rushing flood. Whose breath was unearthly fire. Whose breath would burn a man to death. His face or form was unknown. He would fall upon them like the mountain. He would fall from the face of the rock like the shedding of stone, like an avalanche of heaven, and smother them, crush them.

Gilgamesh turned and looked up as he heard the air, as he felt the air crashing before the weight and he saw, or more truly, he felt the vulnerable moment or knew some flaw in his armor and lifted his sword, determined to kill it as he himself was killed.

The confusion could not be described. Some darkness in turmoil, some terror of noise.

A shedding radiance seared them. A shedding thrice. Like a dark heat, black heat, an oppressive air-sucking heat. And the forest shuddered and was singed. Bracken shriveling, brush blackened, the sacred cedar sap melting ran like blood down the trees and

46

upwardly in lines of blue the precious volatile liquor ignited, streaking up as quickly as it trickled down, and clouds of fragrant incense poured forth from the forest and befogged them.

Then it was gone. Humbaba retreated, wounded, into the forest. Gilgamesh was on his knees, disarmed, and Enkidu unconscious, prostrate on the ground.

Sumerian
Tablets Humbaba hissed: "Let me speak, Gilgamesh. I have no mother. I have no father. I am like the presence of the Mountain that is all that I have ever known. It is she who nurtured me as far as I know and so I keep her. Ellil only knows why. Let me be. Let me go free and I will let you, Gilgamesh, be the only one to possess her and my forest. You may make a palace from my trees."

Gilgamesh was moved with compassion. He thought: "Why should not a bird go free of its snare and return to her nest? Why should not a captive man return to his mother?"

Enkidu spoke to him: "Gilgamesh, the strongest man will fail if he does not use his judgment. Fate that makes no distinction between men will eat him alive. If the snared bird returns to its nest, if the captive man returns to his mother's arms, then my friend will not return to his city."

Humbaba hissed: "Enkidu, you speak evil, you are a beggar for your bread. You only wish to better Gilgamesh. Watch out, Gilgamesh, for his knife in your back."

Enkidu said: "Do not listen, Gilgamesh. Humbaba must die."

But as Gilgamesh replied to Enkidu, still doubtful of his own heart, Humbaba leapt at Enkidu to slay him and Enkidu was thrown, like

47

a leaf by the wind, tumbling like a leaf over and over across the ground, and up the slope of the scree that spilled below the rock face. Gilgamesh felt Humbaba turn toward him, but lay flat and the force of the mountain moved over top of him, like a charging bull whose turned-down horns had blindly missed.

Again the shedding radiance, shedding thrice. The dark heat, the black heat, an oppressive air-sucking heat. And the forest groaned and the sacred cedar sap melting flared and incense befogged them.

Tablet V: Column 3

(Tablets of Nineveh are combined with those of Uruk to make a complete text)

A last assault awaited Gilgamesh, who was disarmed and whose friend now lay battered upon the rocks, was now unguarded and alone, but for the winds of Shamash, that rose with the last light of day, the mountain now purpled with night; but the last winds of day, winds of the sun's last moment, Shamash called them up: Winter winds, Moaning Winds, Western and Eastern, Tempest, Torrent, and Whirlwind; they all converged, thirteen winds in all converged, and Humbaba was darkened against the forest, a blackness in the darkness. He could not charge and he could not run.

Gilgamesh seized his axe and leapt into the blackness and brought down its blade upon the mass of it and Humbaba howled and hurled him away.

Humbaba gasped for breath: "Gilgamesh, you are young. I am not. But I will make the forest grow for you. I will keep the myrtle for your offerings. I will give you cedars for your palace roof."

Enkidu called also to his friend: "Do not listen to his words."

But Humbaba continued: "I should have killed you when I first saw you. You have found the nature of the forest. You know its' magic. Enkidu, I plead to you. It is in your power. We are both children of this mountain. You know we are. Do not let Gilgamesh take my life."

Enkidu stood so that Gilgamesh could hear him. He said: "Kill him now, Gilgamesh. Sever his head. Gut him. Or he shall do it to me. Do it before the gods know what we are about to do. Then we will make an inscription for all men to know, for all men for all time to know, how Gilgamesh slew Humbaba."

Humbaba raised himself to slay Enkidu. His voice deafened them. Enkidu knew he would not live another day.

Enkidu shouted: "Why do you not listen to me Gilgamesh?"

Then Enkidu was silenced, and Humbaba was silenced, and Gilgamesh alone stood upon the body of Humbaba and drew out his entrails.

Then he drew his friend Enkidu away from the great body and revived him.

Humbaba died this way.

The triumph is told, carved on rock taken from the face of this Mountain that stands at the palace of the King of the Four Quarters of the World, so all will remember it.

Humbaba's body they left to carrion birds and other scavengers to eat. They took down forty, fifty trees of whatever they wanted and chose, and hauled them to the river and bound them into rafts that would carry them back to the city of Uruk.[26]

At last Gilgamesh severed the rotting head from Humbaba's body, and hung it from the gate of the forest. Then, as Enkidu guided the rafts down the river, Gilgamesh sat at the edge of the water and washed his weapons and washed the gore of Humbaba out of his hair.[27]

But Enkidu, kin of the cedar forest of Humbaba, feared what they had done and was remorseful. "We have ruined what should not be ruined," he said, without making his voice to be heard.

---

[26] In the Sumerian text the prize of the cedar forest is to be brought to Nippur, rather than Uruk, but then those tablets were found in Nippur.

[27] Sargon of Akkad, it was said, concluded his conquests by washing his gory sword in the Mediterranean Sea—the end of his empire.

Cylinder Seal Impression in Clay
Gilgamesh and Enkidu Slaying Humbaba

NOTE:

Sumerian tablets conclude the episode with the portentous outrage of the god Enlil, guardian and presumed creator of Humbaba, who despairs for his death and who thence imparts the monster's various holy aspects unto the lion, unto the wilderness itself, and unto Ereshkigal (underworld goddess of death).

Enlil (or Ellil in the Akkadian) is a god of unknown origin and uncertain character. He was sometimes called "Great Mountain," and so associated with the Zagros range. He was the patron of the city of Nippur, which was north of Gilgamesh's Uruk, and it is that city from which these Sumerian tablets of this story of Humbaba come.

There is sinister implication to the enduring animosity Ellil feels toward Gilgamesh. This intimation also appears in the recently discovered Babylonian tablet. In the Akkadian versions, however, the persistent subtext concerns Ishtar, which may owe itself to the fact that the bulk of those tablets were found in a city that was the cult center of Ishtar and may have been compiled and recorded by Ishtar's devotees.

The Adventure of the Halub-Tree[28]

Sumerian
Lore

The river Euphrates runs through the park of the temple of Ishtar. In the park, next to the river, there is the Halub-Tree, sacred to Ishtar. She planted it when the world was first created. It has grown there since that day on the river's edge. Ishtar loves this tree.

All manner of birds make homes in it: crane and duck; thrush and Allulu-bird; the hawk even with the sparrow. Her snakes also live amongst her birds.

Its wood is fragrant. It flowers all-over like a meadow; like a high hill with many-colored flowers, it is so huge and wide-spreading.

---

[28] This adventure, as elaborated, is the text of the heavily damaged and mysteriously malapropos twelfth tablet in the Gilgamesh Epic found in the royal library of Nineveh. Its content is disconcerting to scholars as the final chapter to the Epic, because so ranked it would seemingly resurrect Enkidu from the dead for a gratuitous and incoherent conclusion; an end to the Epic with Tablet 11, where Gilgamesh returns to Uruk after his wanderings, seems much more fitting and so nicely closes with an epilogic passage that poetically parallels the prologue in Tablet 1.

But this adventure is a traditional Sumerian tale of Gilgamesh and was appended by the Nineveh compiler for some importance, perhaps as further elucidation of the central theme of death, or rather, the meaning of life in the midst of death. I find its color and its archaic lore mysterious and so include it where other renditions omit it. I have rendered it perhaps more poetically and liberally than my other renditions here, so as to evoke its strangeness. We should remember that in traditional oral storytelling, tales concatenate "spiritually" related matter, even if they are otherwise illogical. Relation, rather than logic, rules the story. Still, in deference to modern narrative sensibilities, I have opted to place the tale among the series of adventures that *precede* the death of Enkidu and the final wanderings of Gilgamesh.

The related and more complete text of the Sumerian lore is included and explicated in the appendix "Gilgamesh, Enkidu and the Nether World."

Bees want to make their honey in it. Gilgamesh sleeps beneath it and his friend Enkidu rests with him.

"Pukku" (stick?) and "mekkû" (hoop?) are used as sport in a sort of field hockey. The game is associated with Ishtar and fertility rituals.

Gilgamesh wanted to make a gift to Ishtar from the wood of the tree. He wanted to give her a chair, hewn whole out of its girth. He wanted to frame and fit a handsome bed out of its great boughs. And with the wood that was left, in her honor too, he would make a *pukku* and *mekkû* for the sports he liked to play, which were also in her honor.

The halub-tree is unidentified. Some suggest it is a willow, others suggest a poplar. Joseph Campbell in his "Oriental Mythology" associated it with the archetypal "world-tree" like the giant ash Yggdrasil of Norse mythology.

Gilgamesh wanted to cut down the Halub-Tree so that it would fall away from the river, back into the park.

But as he struck it, it toppled, completely uprooted, and in the house of its roots a dark deep entrance gaped; the Earth below, where the dead go, opened up to the Earth above where living men are.

Then the tree itself slipped and shuddered, then slid entirely down that hole, like it had been seized, and sank down until the tallest branches were barely seen, going from this world down to the next.

Tablet XII: Column 1

Gilgamesh lamented: "What can I do now to make my *pukku* and *mekkû*? The woodworker will not go down there for me, or his wife will be angry with me. His daughter will be angry with me. Then his wife must be my wife and his daughter must be my little sister."

Enkidu said: "Gilgamesh, my brother,[29] do not be sad, do not cry this way. I will go down and bring up your *pukku* and your *mekkû*."

Gilgamesh warned Enkidu: "If you go down to the Earth,[30] you must follow my instructions. You must not wear clothes that make you stand out. You must not wear perfume or they will smell you and gather around you. Do not startle them. Do not threaten them. Or else the ghosts will collect to you like flies. Do not wear shoes: walk softly and make no noise. If you see them, you must not kiss the wife you love; you must not hit the wife you hate. You must not kiss the son you love. You must not hit the son you hate. For the Earth's outcry will seize you, she who sleeps and sleeps, the mother of Ninazu, who forever sleeps, whose garment's loose about her shoulders and show her breasts, which are like peaches, not the pendulous udders of old women."

Tablet XII: Column 2

Enkidu did not follow his friend's instructions. He put on a clean garment and so they recognized him at once as a stranger. He made too much noise because he wore his shoes. He was anointed with perfumed oil from an ointment jar and so they gathered around at the smell of him. He tossed a stick down in darkness to see what it might hit, it hit them, and so they went after him. He threatened them with a club off the tree and they flew around him like bats.

---

[29] In the Sumerian versions Enkidu is always referred to as "servant" to Gilgamesh, not as friend or brother as he is in the later Babylonian and Akkadian versions. This evolution of their relationship ultimately favors the passionate response by Gilgamesh to his untimely death as later dramatized in the Epic.

[30] The same word, "earth", is used in two senses. Here and in similar context it refers to the Underworld (and even the goddess of the underworld herself); else, it refers to the world above ground where men spend their lives.

When he saw her, he kissed the wife he loved; he hit the wife he hated.

When he saw him, he kissed the son he loved. He hit the son he hated.

And the Earth's outcry seized him, because she who sleeps and sleeps, the mother of Ninazu, who sleeps forever, awoke.

Tablet XII: Column 3 — When Enkidu tried to climb back up again, it was not the Judge of the Dead, Namtar, who stopped him; it was not the demonic Asakku who chased him and held him back. The Earth itself seized him.

The croucher Ukur did not grab his ankle. He did not fall in flight from ghosts. The Earth itself seized him.

When Enkidu did not return, Gilgamesh went to Ellil and complained: "My father, today my *pukku* fell into the Earth. Today my *mekkû* fell into the Earth. Enkidu went down to get them for me. The Earth seized him. It was not Namtar that stopped him; it was not the Asakku that held him back. The Earth itself seized him. The croucher Ukur did not grab his ankle. He did not fall in flight from ghosts. The Earth itself seized him."

Ellil did not answer him, but went alone to the temple of Sin, who is god of the Moon, and he said: "My father, today the *pukku* fell into the Earth. Today the *mekkû* fell into the Earth. Enkidu went down to get them. The Earth seized him. It was not the Judge Namtar that stopped him; it was not the demonic Asakku that held him back. The Earth itself seized him. The croucher Ukur did not grab his ankle. He did not fall in flight from ghosts. The Earth itself seized him."

Namtar is a magistrate of the underworld who decides the fate of men.

Asakku are his demonic agents who police the realm.

Ukur is another demonic deity of the underworld, possibly assimilated with Nergal who is the lover of Ereshkigal, the Queen of the Underworld.

Sin did not answer him, but went alone to the temple of Ea, and he said: "My father, today the *pukku* fell into the Earth. Today the *mekkû* fell into the Earth. Enkidu went down to get them. The Earth seized him. It was not Namtar that stopped him; it was not the Asakku that held him back. The Earth itself seized him. The croucher Ukur did not grab his ankle. He did not fall in flight from ghosts. The Earth itself seized him."

Ea answered. He spoke to Ukur, the consort of the Queen of the Underworld: "Young man, you must open up the passage from the Earth and let Enkidu escape, like a gust of wind he should get loose. Let him return to his brother Gilgamesh."

Ukur did it. He opened the hole and Enkidu escaped like a gust of wind.

Gilgamesh and Enkidu met. They embraced and kissed.

Gilgamesh wondered and wanted Enkidu to tell him, no matter how painful it was: "Tell me, my friend, tell what you found?"

Enkidu said: "I cannot tell you."

Gilgamesh said: "Even if you must weep and be sad, tell me. Did you find your wife? Did you touch her? Weren't you happy to see her? Or had the worms and rats damaged her looks? And your son, how was he? Weren't you happy to see him?"

Enkidu said: "I saw my wife and she was sad and begged me to pity her. I saw my son and he was sad and begged me to pity him.

"I saw many others I knew. One man who wept bitterly. One who had only bread to eat. Another who had only water to drink. One man who was horse driver for them now. Another who is scribe for them now."

[33 lines missing or incomplete]

"One man cries for his mother. Another man I saw is one you know, who died suddenly; he is still lying in his bed, sipping water. I saw one you killed in battle. His father and mother still grieve for him, even there. His wife still weeps for him. I saw one whose corpse was abandoned in the open country. His ghost will not sleep. I saw another one you know whom no one mourns. He has to eat the scraps that other ghosts leave in the street."

And Gilgamesh asked: "Did you see my stillborn children who never knew life? Did you see them? How are they?"

Enkidu replied: "They play at a table that is laden with butter and honey."

Gilgamesh asked: "Did you see the one who died in the fire of his own house? Did you see him? How is he?"

Enkidu replied: "His ghost is not there. His smoke went up to the sky."

All this and more Gilgamesh would know. It is said that Gilgamesh himself, after he had died, becomes a judge in the Underworld where he himself decides such fates for those who die. Gilgamesh cares even for those who have no one to bury them or to speak their names or whose name nobody knows. [31]

---

[31] The last five paragraphs are derived from Dalley's notes about the Sumerian originals. In the Sumerian, as set forth by Heidel, the whole text is set out in repeated rhythmic recitations, alternating Gilgamesh's questions by Enkidu's succinct reply.

The final paragraph is not in the original text but is derived from other legends of Gilgamesh. See Appendix: Death of Gilgamesh.

The Adventure of the Bull of Heaven

Tablet VI:
Column 1

In Uruk Gilgamesh prepared for the temple. He bathed and discarded his clothes. He dressed in fresh clothing and put on a ceremonial robe, closing it with a brilliant sash tied about his waist.

The "Burney Relief," which is believed to represent either Ishtar, the Mesopotamian goddess of love and war, or her older sister Ereshkigal, Queen of the underworld (c. 19th or 18th century BC). Credit: BabelStone

Within the temple Ishtar raised her eyes as he approached and admired him and said: "Come to me, Gilgamesh, and make love to me. Give me the fruit of your body. You will be my husband, I your wife.

"I shall have a chariot inlaid richly with gold and lapis lazuli, with gilded wheels, with crystalline harness, and snowy reins. Horses, whose strength does not fail, like the ocean demons, will take you where you wish.

"Come to me, Gilgamesh. Come to my room fragrant with cedar. The threshold shall kiss your feet. Kings and princes and warriors will bow to you. Mountain orchards shall bear fruit; watered land shall grow much barley. Goats shall bear triplets. Ewes bear twins. Loaded donkeys shall outrun even horses. Horses shall be proud to race. Your ox shall be unrivalled in his yoke."

Gilgamesh made his voice heard and spoke: "What can I give you that you do not already possess? I could give you oil to anoint your body. I could give you garments. I could give you food and drink. But could I give you bread fit for a goddess? Could I give you drink fit for the greatest one? Riches? Or robes? If I were to make love to you, what could I ever give you that is worthy?

Tablet VI: Column 2 "I am not like the others who have loved you. I cannot compare to them. I am just a useless door that cannot keep out the cold. I am a leaky waterskin. I am a bad shoe that hurts the foot.

"I know none of your lovers lasted long. I know none of them lived forever. But I remember them well.

62

Dumuzi is the lover of Ishtar whom she so mourned to lose when he died that she descended to the underworld to be with him. Because of her absence the world wasted away. No fertility existed among men, or animals, or in crops. Thus, she was allowed to return with Dumuzi to the world. The cycle of seasons is explained by the recurrence of this death and resurrection and was celebrated by an annual ritual in Nineveh at which the tablets of the Descent of Ishtar were read aloud.

"Dumuzi, your youthful lover, your first love; you make him weep year after year, even now, taking him, rejecting him, taking him, rejecting him. You also once made love to the colorful Allulu-bird, in the form of lovely youth also, but his wing was broken when he flew away from you. He is in the tree crying: 'My wing! My wing!'

"You loved the lion, whose strength is larger than all, but you dug seven times seven pits for him. You loved the horse, but you make us use whip and lash against him; you make us drive him at full gallop all day long, until he is lathered and thirsty. You decreed the endless weeping of the mother of the horse.

"You loved the shepherd, herdsman and watchman who was always heaping fire for you, and cooked lambs for you every day. But you struck him and changed him into a wolf. His own boys hunted him down and his own dogs tore his haunches with their attack.

Tablet VI:
Column 3

"You loved your father's gardener, Ilshullanu, who brought you each day a new basket of fresh dates. You lifted your eyes to him, as you do to me now, and said to him: 'Let us enjoy ourselves. Put out your hand and touch me here.' And you exposed your vulva to him. But Ilshullanu said: 'Why do you want me? It dishonors you. It

63

dishonors the mother who fed me. I should be left by all society, cold, to live alone in the rushes of the swamp.' He angered you and you struck him too and changed him into a frog, where he lives now among the rushes of the swamp. No more does he draw the water for your garden; no more does he bring the dates to your table.

"So now it is me that you want. How will you treat me? Will you treat me as you have treated them?"

When Ishtar heard Gilgamesh's reply, she was furious with anger and went up to heaven, to Anu, at the Sky's Peak, and wept before her father and her mother, Antu: "Father, Gilgamesh has shamed me again and again, and he taunted me with memories of all of those who dishonored me and hurt me.

Anu heard his daughter and spoke: "Why don't you punish this Gilgamesh yourself, if he has shamed you like you say?"

Ishtar said to her father, Anu: "Give me the Bull of the Heaven[32], Father. Let me destroy Gilgamesh. Let me destroy him where he

---

[32] The Bull of Heaven, associated with the constellation of Taurus (a part of Babylonian astrology which is adopted by the Greeks and Romans), is a recurrent symbol in Near East religious thought, representing the male creative element—force and energy, will and strength. It was also central to the religion of the island of Crete, where the Minoans, who founded the first civilization in the Greek isles before the coming of the Greeks, employed the bull in art, myth, ceremony and sport—in stadiums they vaulted over the heads of charging bulls. The later Roman-era worship of the Bull of Heaven centered on the heroic Mithra who slew the Bull to bring the birth of the world. A similar story is told about Vishnu in Hindu India.

Mithraism was the most popular religion of the Roman soldiers until their gradual conversion to Christianity; to win them over completely, the Roman Catholic church adopted December 25th as the birth date of Christ to take the place of their previous celebration of the birth date of Mithra.

lives. If you do not let me take the Bull of Heaven, I will go down to the underworld, I will bring back the dead; I will bring them into the day light and they will eat all the living. The dead will outnumber the living."[33]

Anu made his voice heard and spoke to his daughter: "On no account should you request the Bull of Heaven from me. There would be seven years of chaff without grain. There would be chalk instead of gems in the mines. There would be weeds instead of wheat."

Ishtar made her voice heard and spoke to her Father: "I have heaped up the storehouses with grain in Uruk. Gems have been taken plentifully. Wheat is abundant there. Let me take the Bull of Heaven."

Tablet VI: Column 4

Anu listened and relented. He put the reins of the Bull of Heaven into her hands. And Ishtar led him to the land of Uruk and she released him and he went down to the riverbed and wandered the seven rivers of the land. At the snorting and stamping of the Bull of Heaven, a chasm appeared beside the river and one hundred young men who were farming or fishing were sucked down into it. Then two hundred. Then three hundred. A second snorting and stamping, and a second chasm swallowed another hundred men, young men, farming or hunting or fishing, and then two hundred more, and then three hundred more. A third snorting

---

[33] This threat to bring the dead back to eat the living, or otherwise destroy creation, is very effective for her. She uses it more than once in Mesopotamian mythology. It is reminiscent of the Indian Goddess Kali who represents both fertility and death, both sexuality and disease. More typically, this paradox and conflict are expressed as two distinct goddesses. Hence, in the Mesopotamian we have Ishtar (for fertility) and Ereshkigal (for death).

and stamping, and a third chasm opened and swallowed another hundred men, young men all, and then two hundred more, then three hundred more.

And in the third chasm Enkidu himself fell. But he leapt out and seized the Bull of Heaven by the horns. The Bull of Heaven blew spittle into his face. With its thick tail, it whipped up its dung. Enkidu made his voice heard and spoke to Gilgamesh: "My friend, we have offended someone. We have insulted them. How can make amends? I will try to hold him but you must plunge your sword into him."

Tablet VI: Column 5   Enkidu was thrown but he seized the tail of the Bull of Heaven and he was tossed as the Bull thrashed his tail, enraged, but Gilgamesh acted skillfully, like a butcher who knows how to slaughter, he plunged his sword in the right place, at the base of the skull, between the tendons of the neck, and the bull collapsed and Gilgamesh and Enkidu began to dress the animal, pulling out his innards.

They put the innards on embers in honor of Shamash and bowed to him, prostrate, and prayerful. Then they fixed the bull to roast upon the fire. Then as two brothers they sat and rested.

Ishtar was furious. She went to the top of the wall of Uruk and shouted curses at them; her face was ugly with anger: "That man Gilgamesh who reviled me has killed the Bull of Heaven."

Enkidu listened to Ishtar and got up and yanked a shoulder of the cooked flesh of the Bull out of its socket and raising it, flung it up at Ishtar, and hit her smack in the face. He called to her: "If I could get to you like that, I would do the same to you with my own hand. I would like to hang his guts on you."[34]

Ishtar gathered her servants from her temple, the harlots, women who worshipped there, the king's own courtesans, and brought them to mourn and weep over the body of the Bull of Heaven.

Meanwhile Gilgamesh called for craftsmen, metal smiths, to come, and they admired the breadth and size of the horns. Thirty minas of lapis lazuli, the sky-blue stone, it took to inlay and encrust the tips of the horns, to make them decorous for drinking horns. Two minas of gold were used to leaf their sheathings. Once complete each could hold six kor of beer.[35]

He dedicated them not to Ishtar, but to his father, Lugalbanda, as a god, to the statue of him that he cared for. He took the horns to his household. In honor of his father, he hung them over the bed where he slept, and near his father's likeness.[36]

Tablet VI: The men washed their hands in the river and went
Column 6   through the street celebrating. The people came out
           and gazed at them. Gilgamesh addressed them:
           "Who is the best among you? Who is the first and
the best man among you? Gilgamesh. Gilgamesh is that man. He is
the only one who can please her, yet turns her away from his bed."

---

[34] This is probably an ironical irreverence, since tokens of entrails as sacrifices to the gods were common, and entrails were employed in sacred prophecy. This is a nastier version of irony than James Joyce's playful heresy in *Ulysses* where the hero changes holy wine into unholy water.

[35] That would be about 950 gallons.

[36] In the original text the "statue" is called "god," as it was the convention to conceive the statue or representation as incarnate of the person or the deity, and so one might speak to it or listen to what it says. The psychological experience is real, even if the devotee recognizes that the statue is not really a god.

Gilgamesh reveled and became drunk in his palace. The whole palace was filled with young men who drank with him and like him finally fell to sleep. And Enkidu also was with them but he fell asleep and had a dream. In his dream he saw the gods consulting. They had gathered and were talking seriously.

Tablet VII: Column 1

With Hittite insertion

When the daylight came Enkidu spoke to Gilgamesh: "My brother, I saw a dream last night. Anu, Ellil, Ea and heavenly Shamash were in the assembly. And Anu said to Ellil 'They have killed the Bull of Heaven; they have killed Humbaba who guarded the Mountain and the Forest of Cedars.' And Anu said: 'One of them must die.' Ellil replied: Let Enkidu die, but let Gilgamesh not die." Then heavenly Shamash said to Ellil, 'Was it not your intent that they kill the Bull of Heaven and Humbaba? For that you would kill Enkidu?' But Ellil was angered and turned to Shamash and said: 'You were their accomplice; like a comrade to them, you helped them.'"

Enkidu knelt, weeping in front of Gilgamesh, and said: "My brother, my brother is so dear to me but they are taking my brother from me."

Hittite insertion ends

And he said: "I shall sit among the dead. I shall pass through the threshold and never again shall I see my brother."

Tablet VII Column 2

Enkidu stood and spoke to the house of Gilgamesh. He addressed the wood of the house, the rafters and the lentils and posts, which he with Gilgamesh had hewn with their own hands, from the Forest of Cedars where Humbaba lived.

68

"I brought you a distance of more than twenty days. There is no other wood like yours. Your length is six poles.[37] This doorpost is made of a single tree. I made you myself. I carried you myself. But tomorrow it will be another who passes under you, another who touch you as I touch you, and someone else will claim to own you, and claim to have made you."[38]

He grasped the frame of the door and wrenched the doorpost from its jamb. He hurled it into the spacious room. Gilgamesh had listened to his friend and now his tears flowed too: "Enkidu, think carefully. Your heart always speaks so calmly. This dream was very precious and the warning awful; I heard you; you murmured as you dreamt, like bees buzzing. The dream is legacy for grief, but is a legacy for next year or many years after. I shall go and offer prayers to the gods. I shall search out your goddess; I shall look for your god, and the father of gods. To Ellil the counselor, father of gods, I shall make a statue; I shall gild it with gold of my own treasure."

Tablet VII Column 3

But the words he spoke did not alter the destiny of Enkidu. The gaming dice cannot be played twice. The words of gods are not forgotten.

At the first light of morning, Enkidu raised his face to Shamash and wept before him: "I beg you, Shamash, let the hunter who first

---

[37] This is about 180 feet high, or the height of a very large pine tree, one that might have grown for perhaps 200 years or more.

[38] Again, in the original Sumerian text, the lumber of the Pine Forest is brought down to Nippur, rather than Uruk. I have omitted that for consistency with the otherwise Akkadian text. See also Note 21. In addition, in the Hittite insertion that I follow here, the text features Ellil's prominent role and the offense to Ellil, rather than the offense to Ishtar whose frustration with Gilgamesh had been the initial pretext for the entire episode. I interpret this apparent inconsistency to represent a divergence in original text; two traditions of religious subtext have become blended.

found me die in misery. And Shamhat too, curse her too, Shamash, for having taken me from my home. I wish she never loves again, never lies with another. I hope disease impregnates her. I hope a drunkard vomits in her lap, her pretty paints become slime. May she sit at the crossroads for her customers all day long and no one ever purchase her. May she lie in the filth of the city, and be a beggar at the gate. And Gilgamesh, he too should suffer. For it is unfair that I who am his equal had none of what he had, and he who is my equal should not have what I am about to have. I hope the builder leaves this house unfinished now.

"I hope the owl nests in your roof and feasts never take place beneath them.[39] Because of you, I lost my home. Because of you, I die."

Shamash heard these prayers and immediately replied with clear and loud voice, called down from the sky: "Enkidu, why to do you curse my harlot Shamhat? She fed you, gave you beer, and clothed you. Then she took you to Gilgamesh so you could be friends and brothers. Now Gilgamesh who will grieve for you as a brother will lay you to bed with loving care; he will keep a vigil and make a lasting dwelling for you, a place for your passage to the other land. Princes will kiss your feet. He will make a mourning day for all of Uruk, and he will weep himself. He will mourn so that he will forget himself, and he will neglect himself, his clothing, and his care for himself. Clothed in a skin of animals he will wander the open country like a man without a family."

---

[39] In Sumerian folklore an owl nesting in one's house forebodes death. The same is said by an ancient Greek folklore. This symbolism of death by the owl is a tradition that is shared by many cultures. To the Algonquin the owl was the guide to the Land of the Setting Sun, the land of the dead. The Maya-Quiche says: "When the owl hoots, the Indian dies."

70

Enkidu heard the voice of Shamash and his heart calmed and anger passed: "Shamash, I change my prayer to you. Instead of curses, make blessings. Shamhat, let me change your fate. Governors and princes shall make love to you. The man with little property shall long for you. The man with much property shall adorn himself for you. The owner of flocks shall not be restrained; he will take from his gown all manner of ivory, of lapis lazuli, of gold, in rings and brooches and bracelets, gifts for you. Rain shall fertilize his fields; his storage jars shall fill for you. The prophet shall lead you to the palace of a king. Because of you he shall forsake his wife of seven years and seven children."

But Enkidu still wept sadly to think of his loss: "I dreamt again, how the sky called out and earth replied and I was between them. There was a young man whose face I could not see clearly, a face like that of Anzu, the sacred bird who must have flown in the sky before there was earth. He had paws of a lion. He had claws of an eagle. He seized me by my locks, and would have taken me away, but I fought him. I hit him. And he could not take me, he kept going up and down like one of those toys that hop about, and he finally struck my head and forced me down. He trampled me like a bull would do. My whole body was crushed beneath him and you did not help me. Now I was like a dove, he took me in his mouth; I was helpless and small.

"He took me down to the dark house, the dwelling of the Largest City, to the dwelling where those who enter cannot ever leave, on the road where the travel is only one way, to the house where those who stay shall have no light, where the dust is their food and clay is their bread. They are clothed like birds, they see no light, and they dwell in darkness. Over the door, on this side of the door, dust has settled; for no one ever opens it.[40]

Tablet VII
Column 6

"I looked at the house that I had entered, and crowns of kings were heaped there and all manner of men made their home there, no matter how important or how rich, or how unimportant or how poor. Some great kings dwelt there. Some great gods dwelt there: Shakkan, the god of cattle; the goddess Ereshkigal, Queen of the Earth; and before her, her scribe Belet-seri kneeling, he was holding a tablet and was reading it to her. She raised her head and looked at me: 'Who brought this man?'"

[The concluding text of the dream is lost;
most of a column is missing]

Gilgamesh had returned from fruitless prayers and Enkidu told him of his dream and said to him: "Remember me, my friend, and do not forget what I have experienced."

From the day that he had this dream his strength diminished. He lay one day, and then on the second the illness grew worse. On the third day and the fourth day he grew weaker. On the fifth, sixth and seventh days, on the eighth, ninth and tenth days he grew weaker still. On the eleventh and on the twelfth days he was almost dead.

---

[40] This paragraph is word for word the opening incantation of the sacred hymn of the Descent of Ishtar in which her entry to the underworld is described. It is typical of literature of an oral tradition, that such verbatim duplication should occur. For in oral traditions, strict recitations are an aid to faithful story-telling, as are recurring catch-phrases and epithets, and parallel repetitions of whole sentences and sequences.

Enkidu lay unconscious in his bed and Gilgamesh beside him at last cried out: "My friend is cursing me. Because in the middle of a fight I was afraid. He was strong and I was a coward." And Gilgamesh wept bitterly.

When the light of dawn appeared on the last day of life for Enkidu, Gilgamesh spoke gently to his friend:

"Enkidu, my friend, your mother was a gazelle, your father a wild horse who sired you. Your milk was from wild asses; they reared you, and the cattle made you familiar with all the pastures. Enkidu's paths led to the Cedar Forest. They shall weep for you night and day, and never be silent. The elders of our city will weep for you. The summit of the temple will bless you. They shall mourn in the open country. They shall mourn in the mountain. Myrtle, cypress and cedar: they shall weep for you, even where we armed ourselves and raged in our fury. Bear, hyena, leopard, tiger, stag, cheetah, lion, wild bulls, deer, goat, cattle and all wild animals: they shall weep for you. The river shall weep, river where we walked together. The water shall mourn for you, the water that we used to drink. All the young men of Uruk, who watched us take down the Bull of Heaven, they will weep for you.

"The ploughman will remember your name. The shepherd and the herdsman will remember. Those who used to make our bread and those who made our beer will remember you. And she shall weep for you, the woman who cared for you, the woman who gave you food and drink, the woman who loved you, and the woman whom you loved: she shall weep for you. And her parents shall weep for you.

"And I, like your father, like your mother, like your wife, I shall weep for you, Enkidu."

Gilgamesh lifted his head: "Listen, young men. Listen, elders of Uruk, listen to me. I myself weep for Enkidu, my friend, my brother, like a woman. I have lost my axe, my sword, my robe and my sash. They are stolen from me.

Tablet VIII
Column 2   "My friend was the leopard of the open country; he was the wild animal that is always free. We met. We took the Mountain of Humbaba. We seized the Bull of Heaven and killed it.

"How can sleep take you away from me? Turn to me.

"Why aren't you listening to me?"

But Enkidu did not lift his head. Gilgamesh touched his heart and it did not beat at all.

So the face of Enkidu was covered with a veil like a bride's, and Gilgamesh withdrew.

He paced in the palace, back and forth like a lioness whose cubs are trapped in a pit below her. He tore out his hair with anguish. He tore the fabric of his clothing. He cast away all that the things that he cherished as if they were taboo.

When the dawn appeared, Gilgamesh sent out a shout throughout the land. Smith, coppersmith, silversmith, jeweler were summoned and he ordered them to make a likeness of his friend, to make a statue of him, to be an immortal god of him. Skin of gold they gave him and limbs of and body of lapis lazuli.

[A short gap in the text here; then
a good deal of the final few columns in

74

this tablet are damaged beyond recognition; so this is much abbreviated and somewhat conjectural]

Tablet VIII
Column 3

"I will lay you to your bed with love. And you will stay in this dwelling safely, a place with passage to the other land. Princes of the earth will kiss your feet. The people of Uruk shall take a day of mourning for you. And I will neglect myself in mourning for you. Clad in the skin of an animal I will leave this city, and I will wander the open country like a man without a family."

When first light came, Gilgamesh undid the fittings of his garments and prepared for the temple. He bathed and discarded his clothes. He dressed in fresh clothing and put on a ceremonial robe, closing it with a brilliant sash tied about his waist.

He ordered his tributes for Enkidu. He gave his treasure for his memory. Then he made libation to Shamash but he could not speak, his sorrow was so heavy.

He made his offerings to Shamash and at last admitted his grief: "I would gladly go with him to be at his side."

He performed the funerary rites for Enkidu, as would the priest of the temple, anointing his statue with affection, filling the lapis lazuli bowl with butter, filling the carnelian bowl with honey. He decorated the statue of Enkidu and showed it to Shamash. And when he had finished, he left the temple; he left the city of Uruk.

He removed his rich garments and wearing only the skins of animals he went into the open country to roam like a man without a family.[41]

---

[41] Gilgamesh has assumed the "primitive" circumstance that Enkidu himself possessed before he was transformed to his "human nature" by Shamhat. His wanderings, like those of Odysseus, take him beyond the realm of the mankind, beyond the realm of the world. But Gilgamesh renounces society and human endeavors, whereas Odysseus seeks to return to them. Gilgamesh is disillusioned and morbid; he seeks a renewal or a justification for a life that has been disfigured by suffering, disappointment and vanity. As a legend, Gilgamesh shares more with the life of the Buddha, who was preoccupied with the objective of transcendence and enlightenment, than it shares with the legends of Greek and Roman heroes whose lives were preoccupied with mastery and achievements.

The Wanderings of Gilgamesh

Tablet IX
Column 1

Gilgamesh mourned bitterly the death of his friend Enkidu and roamed the open country.

"Shall I die? Am I not just like Enkidu? Grief possesses me; it has entered me deeply. I am like a ghost that cannot go down and roams the open country."

So he took the road to Ut-napishtim, son of Ubara-Tutu; he looked for Ut-napishtim because he is the only man who has not yet died.

Babylonian
(Meissner)
Tablet X (?)
Column 1

He roamed the country like a man without family, like a ghost who cannot go down. Wherever the winds chase. Wherever the waters go. He did not cease to travel. He did not sleep.

Shamash was worried and came to him at the end of the day. He spoke to him: "Gilgamesh, where are you going? You will not find a life that does not die."

Gilgamesh replied to Shamash, the warrior: "Though I go traveling restlessly now, there will be no lack of sleep after I die. Why should I sleep now? Let my eyes fill with light. I want to see the sun. Do dead men see the sun? The darkness is empty; where is the light then?"

Tablet IX
Column 1
(resumed)

He reached the mountain passes at night. He saw lions there and was afraid. He raised his head and prayed to the moon in her tribal name, Sin, who lights the unvoiced thoughts of gods: "Keep me safe."

He slept uncomfortably, worried, and awoke at a dream and was glad to be alive. A pack of menacing predators—lions or hyenas or others—surrounded him. He took up his ax, and drew his sword and like an arrow, he charged them. He shattered the skull of one and the others ran.

[13 damaged lines]

The name of the mountain is Mashu. Mashu protects the daily departure of Shamash. The roof of the Sky is braced upon it, supported upon its weight and strength, like a lintel. A mantle of frightening radiance is all about the mountain.

The place is guarded by scorpion-men. Their presence is terrifying; a glance of their eyes can mean death. They soldier the place at dusk and dawn.

Fear clouded Gilgamesh as he looked at them. But he took initiative. He gestured to them in friendship and greetings.

Tablet IX
Column 2
A Scorpion-man shouted to his woman: "Look. Someone has come. He has the flesh of one of the gods."

The Scorpion-man's woman answered: "He is only partly god. He is also mortal."

The Scorpion-man challenged Gilgamesh: "Who are you? What distance have you come?"

[14 damaged lines]

Gilgamesh told him of his long journey, the difficulties of the mountain passes, and how he looked for Ut-napishtim who alone of all men has not yet died.

The Scorpion-man made his voice heard and spoke: "It is impossible, Gilgamesh. Nobody passes through the Mountain of Mashu down the cavern of the sun. After a distance of two or three hours, the darkness has become so dense, you cannot see."

Tablet IX
Column 3   [41 damaged or missing lines]

Gilgamesh looked gaunt with fatigue, like that of a man who has traveled too far from home and is exhausted and haunted by grief.

The Scorpion-man made his voice heard and spoke: "If you must go, Gilgamesh, this is the entrance to the cavern here; you can see the course of Shamash by the luminance that trails behind him. But it is impossibly dark in its depths."

Tablet IX   Gilgamesh departed and did not look back until four
Column 4   hours of journey but then he could not see where he
              had come from. He could not see what was ahead.

[8 damaged or missing lines]

Tablet IX   He hurried into the darkness. In two more hours the
Column 5   darkness was still dense. There was no light. He
              could not see ahead or behind. He hurried on for
              two more hours. Still there was no light. The
darkness was dense. He could not see ahead or behind.

At ten hours, at twelve hours, there still was no light in the cavern. But he did not hesitate. The darkness was so dense, he could not see ahead or behind.

But at the fourteenth hour he came out suddenly into the light, the sun was in front of him; brightness was everywhere and all kinds of thorny, spiky bushes, blossoming with gemstones. Carnelian was fruit on some, hanging in gleaming clusters; lapis lazuli was the foliage in others, fruited also, and delightfully sparkling.

[24 damaged or missing lines]

Tablet IX
Column 6
Pine of jade arose above him. Fronds of the white pappardilu-stone spread as undergrowth, and brambles and thorn-bushes of the green abasmu-stone, of the subu-stone, of hematite. Riches, wealth abounded; turquoise stones dropped like dates.

As Gilgamesh walked around in wonder, he saw distantly the alewife, tavern keeper, Siduri, who lives alone by the sea that edges the world.

Siduri, the alewife, lives at the sea on the edge of the world and keeps a tavern there. Vats of beer in fermentation stand there, covered so that they are not polluted. Gilgamesh circled it carefully, wearing his animal skins, for though he has the flesh of the gods, he is not a god.[42]

---

[42] The profession of alewife, as Dalley relates in her footnotes, is referenced in Mesopotamian law, including the Code of Hammurabi. Her's was a service to long-distance trade at remote stations along the established roads and at the frontiers. The alewife was a woman of property who was independent of the usual male social prerogatives, but who was sponsored by the rulers of a patron city that had some interest in the trade she supported. Her beer and ales came from the patron city or at least her grains for fermentation did. In an Akkadian list the name "Siduri" is associated with Ishtar as a goddess of wisdom.

Tablet X
Column 1

Grief possessed him; it had entered him deeply. He was like a ghost that cannot go down and roams the open country.

The alewife saw him from the distance, and watched him approach. She pondered in her heart. She spoke to herself: "This man looks like a bad man. Why does he come here looking like he does?"

She went inside her tavern and she locked her door to him. She bolted it. Gilgamesh saw and when he came closer he spoke to her: "Why did you lock your door?"

"I will break it open if I must. I have traveled a great distance. I am Gilgamesh, brother of Enkidu. We killed Humbaba in the Forest of Cedars. We killed the Bull of Heaven that came up the river into the city of Uruk."

The alewife did not believe him: "If you are really Gilgamesh, who slew the Guardian Humbaba that lived in the Forest of Cedars, who killed the lions at the mountain pass, who seized and struck down the Bull of Heaven, then why are your cheeks so wasted, your face so dejected, your body so worn, and your clothing so shabby? You look possessed of a sorrow that has entered you deeply. Your face is gaunt, like that of a man who has traveled too far from home and is exhausted and haunted by grief."

Tablet X
Column 2

Gilgamesh spoke to her through the door: "How should it not be? My cheeks are wasted, my heart wretched, my appearance worn out. Grief has entered me deeply. My face is weathered by heat and cold and is gaunt like that of a man who has traveled so far from home and is exhausted. My friend, my brother, Enkidu, who

81

shared my life with me, was taken away from me, dead, as all die. Six days, seven nights I wept. I did not want him buried. Not until a worm fell of out of his nose. Then I was frightened too. And afraid of death, defeated by it too, I roamed the open country like a ghost that cannot go down. No longer king. I wear these animal skins. The words of my friend—"Remember me"—haunt me. Wherever I go these words go with me in my mind.

"How can I accept this? My friend is cold and lifeless. Won't this be my fate too? I will lie down someday and never again get up."

Babylonian (Meissner) Tablet X (?) Column 3   The alewife spoke to him, to Gilgamesh: "What you want you cannot have. You will not find a life that does not die. When mankind was created by the gods, they kept undying life for themselves; they gave death to man.

"So, Gilgamesh, fill your stomach. Enjoy yourself. Take pleasure every day and every night in every way you can. Play. Dance. Refresh yourself with baths. Wash your hair. Put on clean clothes. Take your child's hand in yours and take your wife on your lap. That is life."

Gilgamesh replied: "I do not understand anything you say or why you say it. My heart hurts with grief for my friend. That is all I know. You must know the way to Ut-napishtim; you see all types here who come and go at the edge of the sea."

Tablet X Column 2 (resumed)   Gilgamesh insisted: "Tell me, Alewife, which way is the way to Ut-napishtim? Can you give me directions? Whatever they are, I will take them. If I must, I shall cross this sea. But if that is not possible, I shall go back and wander the open country again."

82

The alewife opened her door and spoke to him: "There has never been a ferry of any kind, Gilgamesh. No one has ever crossed the sea and come back alive. Shamash, who is a warrior like you, is the only one who crosses the sea. Apart from him, no one else. The crossing itself is difficult and the way of it difficult. In between this world and the next world are the Waters of Death, a barrier none can pass. How should even you, Gilgamesh, ever hope to do it?

"But if you must there is a boatman, Ur-shanabi, who works for Ut-napishtim. He goes to him from time to time and even now is in the forest trimming a pine for him. Go, speak to him, and see if it is possible to cross with him. Otherwise, you must turn around and go back."

Gilgamesh went down to the seashore, to where the mountain met the sea and pines grew nearby. He went armed in case he should be threatened.

Ur-shanabi saw him coming, drew out his own sword and raised up an ax, and crept up behind Gilgamesh. But Gilgamesh was swift and sure and struck Ur-shanabi, struck him down, and seized his arms behind him and pinned him to the ground. He bound his arms. Gilgamesh was furious at Ur-shanabi, and he threw his sword into the water, and destroyed other things that were near about. There were peculiar things of stone, strung with rope, like floats and nets that a fisherman might cast. He smashed them. He made dust out of them and the rope was all unstrung from them. He even would have made a hole or two in his boat but he had the sense to stop. He went back to Ur-shanabi.

Tablet X
Column 3

Ur-shanabi spoke to Gilgamesh: "Why are your cheeks so wasted, your face so dejected, your body so worn, and your clothing so shabby? You look possessed of a sorrow that has entered you deeply. Your face is gaunt, like that of a man who has traveled too far from home and is exhausted and haunted by grief."

Gilgamesh replied: "How should it not be? My cheeks are wasted, my heart wretched, my appearance worn out. Grief has entered me deeply. My face is weathered by heat and cold and is gaunt like that of a man who has traveled so far from home and is exhausted. My friend, my brother, Enkidu, who shared my life with me, was taken away from me, dead, as all die. Six days, seven nights I wept. I did not want him buried. Not until a worm fell of out of his nose. Then I was frightened too. And afraid of death, defeated by it too, I roamed the open country like a ghost that cannot go down. No longer king. I wear these animal skins. The words of my friend—"Remember me!"—haunt me. Wherever I go these words go with me in my mind.
"How can I accept this? My friend is cold and lifeless. Won't this be my fate too? I will lie down someday and never again get up."

Gilgamesh insisted: "Tell me, Ur-shanabi, which way is the way to Ut-napishtim? Can you give me directions? Whatever they are, I will take them. If I must, I shall cross this sea. But if that is not possible, I shall go back and wander the open country again."

Ur-shanabi told him then: "You have almost made it impossible yourself. Those things of stone that you smashed keep you safe in the Waters of Death, but they are destroyed and all unstrung, and I do not know if you can survive it now. But if you must you can try to go by taking poles and like a ferryman make your way, like a boatman in the river, using poles to go. Cut down the poles from trees—three hundred you will need—and shape them, hew them with a place to handle them, then bring them here to my boat."

Gilgamesh went to the forest and took down three hundred trees and trimmed them, hewed them and made a handle on each of them. When he was done, he hauled them to the boat where Ur-shanabi waited. They boarded and embarked together. They cast a sail and the wind took them into the sea.

After a journey of a new moon to a full moon, and three more days besides, they reached the Waters of Death, where there was no wind, a shoal of lifeless emptiness, in which the overcast sky reflected upon the sea colorlessly.

Tablet X
Column 4

"Don't let the water wet your hand," Ur-shanabi told Gilgamesh. "Hold the pole high and thrust it once. Then take another and thrust it. Then a third. Then another and so on. One by one. But do not touch the water."

In less than one half mile, no more, he had used up all his poles. He had no more.

But the boat drifted smoothly. The boat glided in the straight course he had given.

Ut-napishtim was on the other shore. He looked out for them. He was puzzled. He could see his boatman. But he could see another also "I am looking, but I cannot believe it. I am looking but I cannot make it out."

[Gap of 20 lines or so]

Tablet X
Column 5

Ut-napishtim addressed Gilgamesh as all had before: "Why are your cheeks so wasted, your face so dejected, your body so worn, and your clothing so shabby? You look possessed of a sorrow that has entered you deeply. Your face is gaunt, like that of a man who

85

has traveled too far from home and is exhausted and haunted by grief."

Gilgamesh replied: "How should it not be? My cheeks are wasted, my heart wretched, my appearance worn out. Grief has entered me deeply. My face is weathered by heat and cold and is gaunt like that of a man who has traveled so far from home and is exhausted. My friend, my brother, Enkidu, who shared my life with me, was taken away from me, dead, as all die. Six days, seven nights I wept. I did not want him buried. Not until a worm fell of out of his nose. Then I was frightened too. And afraid of death, defeated by it too, I roamed the open country like a ghost that cannot go down. No longer king. I wear these animal skins. The words of my friend—"Remember me!"—haunt me. Wherever I go these words go with me in my mind.

"How can I accept this? My friend is cold and lifeless. Won't this be my fate too? I will lie down someday and never again get up."

And Gilgamesh added at last: "So I thought I must go see Utnapishtim, the far-distant man, whom all the people tell me about. I searched; I went to all the countries that I knew. I passed through open country, mountains, all manner of difficult land, and crossed seas, back and forth. I never slept enough. My body was anxious all the time. What did I find? Did I gain anything? I killed bear, hyena, lion, leopard, and the tiger. I ate their meat. I skinned them and spread their skin and now I wear them. I ate and skinned the deer, the goat, cattle and other wild animals.

"I tried to get the help of the alewife but she was afraid of me, she thought I must be a bad man because of how I looked. She bolted her door against me.

"Now no one has pleasure when I am near. My misery makes misery wherever I am."

[About 16 lines that are damaged]

Tablet X
Column 6

Ut-napishtim said to Gilgamesh: "Why do you make your grief worse? Because the gods made you flesh? Because you are like your father and your mother? Death must come to you, to you and to any idiot, Gilgamesh. A throne is given to you. A idiot gets a stool. You get butter. The idiot gets rancid dregs. He gets a loincloth: you get a robe. He has no sense: you get advice from wise men.

"You have appeared to gods. You have cared for temples and holy shrines. The gods have listened to you. So what have you achieved? Why do you do all this?

"You are weary and exhausted. You have filled yourself with grief. You only bring the distant day of death that much closer to you.

"Even fame is cut down like the reed in its bed. A fine man, a fine girl will die like flowers cut. Nobody sees death coming. Nobody hears death coming. Death cuts down the living like the reeds in the river bed.

"We build a house. We build a farm. When the old man dies, the brothers divide it. There is hostility between them.

"The river rises and brings the floods. The dragonflies drift on the river. Their faces look upon the face of the sun. Suddenly there is nothing.

"The sleeping and the dead are just alike. No one can picture death. No one knows more than a man who knows nothing.

"Even when they blessed me, the Anunnaki, the assembly of gods, they appointed life and death. They did not make a number to count the days of death, but they do count all the days of life. Those days are the only ones that you must count."

Tablet XI
Column 1 Gilgamesh spoke to Ut-napishtim the far distant: "I look at you and I see a man not much older than I am. You have the arms of a man my age. It makes me want to prove myself against you. How is this so? Because I know you must be many thousands of years older than I."

Ut-napishtim said to Gilgamesh: "I will tell the secret. It is a secret of the gods themselves and men have not known it until today.

"You know the city Shuruppak, on the bank of the Euphrates. That city was very old when I was young. The gods decided they should make a flood. Anu, the father of them; and Ellil who is warrior and counselor; and Ninurta who is his chamberlain; and Ennugi their canal-manager. Ea, far-sighted, made them all swear an oath in secrecy about their plot, so that no man alive would know.

"But in order to tell me, but not break his oath, he, Ea himself, spoke to my hut, to the walls of my hut. I heard him when I was inside of it. He said: 'Listen, reed hut. Listen to me brick and brick wall. Pay attention, wall. I want you to tell the man of Shuruppak, son of Ubara-Tutu, to take down these walls, and build a boat. Leave these possessions, but search out all living things. Reject property, but save the lives. Put aboard the boat the seed of all living things. The boat you build shall be equally long as wide, these dimension shall be balanced. Roof her like the sky, her entire length and breadth.'

Ea who tells Ut-napishtim about the coming flood is one of the most ancient gods of Mesopotamia and always beneficent to mankind. He represents fresh water and was the intermediary to the seven sages who brought the arts of civilization to man. He is also invoked as a god of wisdom and incantations. His symbols include an overflowing vase, the horned crown and a goat-fish. His epithet is "far-sighted."

Tablet XI
Column 2

"I realized I spoke to my master Ea, and I paid close attention to his words. I asked him: 'Master, I shall do as you say, but how shall I explain myself to other people, and the elders and men of the city.'

"Ea made his voice heard and spoke to me: 'You will tell them this—that you cannot stay in the city any longer, that you cannot tolerate the land of Ellil any longer, but you must go down to the sea, out to the sea of first creation, and stay with your master Ea. There he will shower abundance on you, fowl and fish, a treasure, a harvest.

"In the morning, you will have cakes. In the evening, you will have wheat. In the morning, clouds gather. In the evening, rain falls. [43]

"When the light of dawn appeared, the men who lived near about me had gathered around my house and I asked the carpenter to come. The reed worker came and brought his scythe, and young men helped me haul in the

---

[43] Among the literary devices that are favored by the Epic are the double entendre, or pun, homonyms that suggest parallel meanings. So earlier we identified epithets for Enkidu that also are names of Ishtar's temple attendants. Here Dalley notes the pun between words for "cakes" and "clouds" and then words for "wheat" and "rain." Thus, what I am obliged to render by four sentences are only two in the native text.

89

timber, and tar, and other materials that I needed.[44] Slaves and even children carried what they could. By the fifth day, I had laid out her structure. A whole acre would be the area of her deck. A length of not less than ten poles she was from stern to stem.[45] Across the beam she was ten poles. I gave her six decks and divided these by seven spaces. I saw to the rudder. I put down all that was needed.

"Three sar of bitumen I poured into the kiln. Three sar of pitch I poured into the inside. Three sar of oil the workmen fetched by basket. Not counting the sar of oil which earthen matting soaked up, they stored away two more sar of oil.

"I gave them all ointment for their hands at the start of each day's work. At day's end I slaughtered oxen for a great meal and gave the workmen beer and ale to drink all day long. It was a feast, like New Year's day, and I sacrificed a sheep each day. Then one sundown the boat was done.

"It was difficult to launch her. The rollers had to be fetched from above and placed below to advance her to the river. Once I had at least one-third of her in the water, I began to load her. I loaded everything there was. Silver things. Gold things. Seed of all living things. All my kith and kin went on the boat. Cattle from the open country went on the boat. All kinds of craftsmen.

"Shamash had fixed the hour: 'In the morning cakes (darkness); in the evening wheat (rain).' I saw the shape of the storm coming. It was terrifying to see. I boarded and closed the gangway. She was a

---

[44] The boat described is like the flat boats used on the river travel, built like rafts with lashings, matting, tarred and tied. Only this one is immense and perhaps a bit more boat-like than most. Sumerians did build sea-faring craft but even these employed the same materials.

[45] 1 pole = 30 feet; 3 sar = 24,000 gallons.

90

floating palace. She was an enormous storehouse. I turned steerage over to my boatman.

"When the dawn came, the clouds gathered darkly at the base of sky. The gods rumbled inside of it. Others marched, advancing like enemies within it. The weirs and ditches overflowed. The moorings of other boats pulled out. The light of day quailed. All went dark. Even the gods wanted light to see. There was a moment's calm before the storm overwhelmed us. Then the tempest rose and brought the torrent and the flood, like a weapon, like an enemy with weapons, it passed among the people and rushing through the city, it killed them all. No one could see another in the darkness and the terror. The earth and sky were flooded alike and even the gods were afraid and withdrew. They cowered beyond the world, like dogs behind a wall, and Ishtar screamed like a woman giving birth. Our mistress of gods, sweet voice, was wailing: 'Has time reversed? Is all gone back to clay? I spoke evil with the gods. How could I have spoken that evil with you? I should have taken you to battle for this. I myself gave birth to these; they are my own children. Now they fill the sea like fish dying in their spawn!'

"The gods of Anunnaki were weeping with her. Humbled and ashamed, they wept. They were speechless. They could only watch in horror. For six days and seven nights the wind blew, the flood and tempest overwhelmed the lands. On the seventh day after the tempest had come—flood, onslaught that howled like a woman in labor—the winds faded, and the sky cleared. The sea became calm and blue. And wind became a zephyr, gentle and pleasant. Still the lands were flooded everywhere.

"I looked out from the boat. Silence reigned. All mankind was gone. The plains of our lands were flooded everywhere and all was flat as a roof. I opened the window of my house on the deck and sunlight touched my cheek. I looked out, saw and wept. I looked for banks, for limits to the sea; there were none.

Tablet XI Column 4

"The boat came to rest against the slopes of Nimush, the mountain, and did not move from there. Three days, then the fourth it was held fast. A fifth and sixth day and still it did not move. When the seventh day came, I released a dove. The dove went and came back. No perching place had it found and so it turned back. I put out a swallow and it came back. I put out a raven and it saw the waters receding and it ate, preened its feathers, and did not turn around. So I released all my birds and made sacrifice to the gods. I set out a smoke-offering on the mountain peak. I arranged seven pots, seven by seven pots in the embers, and I poured oils of myrtle, reeds and pine. The gods smelled the fragrance and gathered like flies over the sacrifice. As soon as Ishtar came, she saw the swarming of the gods that Anu had gathered and said: 'I shall never forget. I shall never forget these times. All gods may enjoy this offering, except Ellil, never Ellil, because he did not ask before bringing the flood and destroying my children.'

"When Ellil did come, and he saw the boat with all of us, and all the living creatures, he was furious. He was angry especially with the gods of his own generation: 'Who survived? What life has survived? Nothing should have survived!'

"Ninurta, his own son who used to help us with our agriculture and our wars, he said to his father: 'Ea must have done this. Only Ea could have done this.'

"Ea did make his voice heard and he spoke to Ellil: "You are wise, and a warrior, Ellil. How could you fail to ask us before you did this? Punish the sinner for his sin. Punish the criminal for his crime. But do not destroy all living things for this. Be patient and

92

let this be. Instead of condemning it to destruction, instead of imposing this flood, you should let the lion diminish them. Let the wolf diminish them. Let the famine diminish them. Let even war or plague savage them, if you must. I did not tell the secrets of the gods, but it is true that Atrahasis[46] had a dream in which I spoke and so he heard the secret of the gods.'

"Ea's counsel prevailed in the assembly and Ellil came over to my boat and seized my hand and brought me forward and he led my woman up and made her kneel beside me. Standing between us he touched both our foreheads and blessed us: 'Until now Ut-napishtim was mortal, but henceforth he and his woman shall be as we gods are. Ut-napishtim shall dwell far off, beyond the mouth of the rivers on the edge of the world.'

"So they took me and made me dwell far away from mankind. So, you see, Gilgamesh, I cannot help you; I cannot bring the gods together, as they gathered for me, so that you too can have life without dying."

"But if you wish it, then like me, you must first do this: you too must not sleep for six days and seven nights. Then we shall see."

Gilgamesh attempted, but as soon as he was sitting, his chin on his knees, sleep clouded him like the fog. Ut-napishtim spoke to his

---

[46] The name of Ut-napishtim before he was made "immortal" was Atrahasis, and by that hero's name most of the Epic's audience would have known this tale of the Flood. The use of the name "Ut-napishtim" appears to be a deliberate and artful representation by the "author" of this Epic, being a literal translation of the much older Sumerian name for the original hero of the Flood, meaning "he who lives long." This, and some other evidently consciously thematic constructions, makes strong argument that the Epic of Gilgamesh is truly literary, an intelligently written work like a novel, rather than a mere compilation recounting folklore by rote. See Appendix for more discussion of the Epic as literature.

wife and said: "See this young man who wants eternal life. He cannot stop the sleep that clouds him like a fog."

His wife replied: "Touch him. Wake him up. Let him go back in peace to where he came from. He should go through the gate to his own land."

Tablet XI
Column 5 Ut-napishtim spoke to his wife: "This man behaves badly. I will not wake him. Bake his daily portion of bread and put it here by his head as he sleeps. Mark along the wall the number of days that he sleeps by the number of loaves of bread you place along it."

She baked a portion of bread for him daily and placed it by his head, in a row along the wall. His first day's portion was stinking. The second had discolored, the third had white mould, the fourth was soggy, the fifth was going bad, the sixth was dried out, and the seventh was just coming out of the oven—at that moment Ut-napishtim touched him and Gilgamesh awoke. Gilgamesh spoke: "Why did you wake me? I have not been asleep at all."

Ut-napishtim said: "Look, Gilgamesh, count your daily portions. That number of days you have slept. The first is stinking. The second is discolored. The third has white mould. The fourth is soggy. The fifth is going bad. The sixth is dried out. Now you are awake and your bread is coming out of the oven"

Gilgamesh said to Ut-napishtim: "How could I have done this? What will happen to me now? The stalkers wait on the road. Death waits in my bedroom. Wherever I go, Death is there."

In anger Ut-napishtim addressed Ur-shanabi the boatman: "You can never come here again. Our harbor will cast you back to the sea; the ferry will turn you away. Because of this man.

94

"Take him away with you. His hair is filthy and his body suffers. Take him; bring him a basin to wash with and let him bathe. Throw the rotten skins he wears into the sea. Let him soak until he is refreshed. Put a new headband about his clean hair. Give him a robe to wear so that he may be proud of himself again. Then he may return home proudly and this garment shall not fade but shall look just as new as it is when he reaches his home."

Ur-shanabi took him and brought him a basin to wash with. And he washed his filthy hair. He took away his skins and the sea carried them off. His body was soaked until he was refreshed. He put on a new headband. He put on a new robe that made him proud of himself. The garment will not fade but will still look new when he returns home.

Gilgamesh and Ur-shanabi now went to the sea to prepare the boat to sail. They raised the sail and the winds rippled them. They stood in the boat ready to depart.

Ut-napishtim's woman spoke to her husband: "Gilgamesh has come seeking something and is weary with his life. What will you give him to take back to his country?"

Tablet XI
Column 6

Ut-napishtim spoke to Gilgamesh: "You came seeking something, Gilgamesh, and are weary with life. So what is it that I can give you? I will give you a secret. Only the gods know this. There is a plant whose stalk is thorny, whose thorns will spike your hands. It you can win that plant, you will find rejuvenation."

Ut-napishtim told him where and how to gain this plant. We are forbidden to know it. So it is not told. Gilgamesh set sail in a boat. Ur-shanabi took him because he was an outcast and could never

95

Apsu is one of two primordial beings out of which all-else flows. The other, Tiamat, represents what we call "chaos." Apsu in marriage to it can cause creation. Apsu is fresh water. Tiamat is salt water.

"When the skies were not yet named nor earth below pronounced by name, Apsu, the first one, their begetter, and the maker Tiamat, who bore them all, mixed their waters together...."
— The Epic of Creation

return. Somewhere in the very midst of the sea—we do not know where—they stopped. Gilgamesh followed the instructions of Ut-napishtim—what they were we do not entirely know.

The ritual and instruments of ritual that he held, he used exactly as he should; except in one way, all was as it should be. [47]

He tied heavy stones to his feet. He jumped into the sea, like a man who wanted to end his life. To the depths he went, to the depths of Apsu, where are the first fresh waters that flow from the center of the world, where the Seven Sages once dwelt, where that is which fills emptiness, and there he found the plant. He took the plant and it spiked his hands. He cut the stones from his feet and the sea threw him up on the shore.

Gilgamesh called back across the sea to Ur-shanabi who sailed the boat to shore; he told him what he had found: "Ur-shanabi, this

---

[47] This is a stylistic representation of the fact that, although it is not corrupted or missing words, the text seems to be missing most details. While we might normally have expected repeated recitations of these details—first, as the instructions and then, as the actions, as in other such narrative passages of the *Epic*—here the details are simply omitted or deliberately obscure. Among later Mystery religions that were widely distributed and greatly popular throughout the Hellenistic world, including what is native Mesopotamia, omissions or obscurities such as these are meant to disguise and protect secrets that may not be spoken to any but initiates, and so we have followed the implication of secrecy. The fragmentary original here and later at the conclusion contains obscure references to some ritual or magical instruments.

plant is a plant of miracles! The breath of life comes back to one who is given it. I will take it back to Uruk. I will try it on an elder to see how well it works, and then I will try it too and I shall be the young man that I once was. I will call this plant, "An-old-man-grows-into-a-young-man."

They found themselves on the shore of the sea, near the mouth of the rivers, and so they did not have far to go, taking the boat now up the river to Uruk. For two days they went before they stopped to eat. On the third day they finally stopped to rest for a night's sleep.

Gilgamesh saw an inlet of cool water at the riverside and went to the water to wash. He set down the plant and a snake smelled the fragrance of the plant. It came silently out of the water and carried the plant away in its mouth, swallowing it. As it slithered into the water, Gilgamesh saw how it shed its skin.

Gilgamesh sat down and wept. Tears flowed down his cheeks: "For what purpose, Ur-shanabi, have my arms grown weary? Why does the blood in my body still keep me alive?

"I have gained nothing. This beast of the earth takes it and is gone. The current carries it to the sea and soon it will be back where it came from. I should have known: while I was preparing to take it, something went wrong; it was an omen to me." Gilgamesh lifted his face: "It is finished."[48]

---

[48] *"Consummatum est,"* as Marlowe's Faustus said when he signed away his soul to Mephistopheles, as Christ said when he died upon the Cross. The search ends here. Heidel translates it: "I will withdraw." Dalley translates it: "I shall give up." Sandars translates it: "I have lost it."

They left the boat on the shore. For two days they went before they stopped to eat. On the third day they finally stopped to rest for a night's sleep.

Then they reached Uruk, the Sheepfold. Gilgamesh spoke to Urshanabi: "It is I who built up the wall of Uruk, which shines like a copper band, surrounding the holiest shrine, Sheepfold of Eanna, House of the Sky, the home of Ishtar.

"Look along the long line of its high battlements—no one will ever match them. Come up to its gateway that has stood since before anyone can remember. Look at the wall I built; these are baked bricks; it is so well built only the first men, the Seven Councilors who taught us all our skills, could have laid this foundation.

"Inside this wall there lies one square mile that is city, one square mile that is orchards, one square mile that is clay pits, and then the open ground for Ishtar and her temple. These four parts: that is the city of Uruk."

So, it is written and corrected by this scribe: this is Gilgamesh, the man who found out all things, he who experienced everything, he who searched everywhere, and gained complete wisdom. He found out what was secret and uncovered what was hidden. He brought back the tale of times before the Flood. He journeyed far and wide, until weary and at last resigned.

Background Discussions:

Background on Sources of Text

This "retelling" is derived from the literal English translations of the tablets by three principal sources:

- *The Electronic Text Corpus of Sumerian Literature @* http://www-etcsl.orient.ox.ac.uk/, Copyright 2003, 2004, 2005, 2006 The ETCSL project, Faculty of Oriental Studies: Black, J.A., Cunningham, G., Fluckiger-Hawker, E, Robson, E., and Zólyomi, G.,University of Oxford

- the definitive Akkadian texts translated by Stephanie Dalley in her *Myths from Mesopotamia: Creation, The Flood, Gilgamesh, and Others*, Oxford University Press: Oxford, 1989; and

- *The Epic of Gilgamesh and Old Testament Parallels*, Alexander Heidel, University of Chicago Press: Chicago, 1963.

All translated text is heavily interpolated. Often the text is reconstructed from many "manuscripts" or versions, various tablets or fragments of tablets that have been found in various locations from various epochs, and these sometimes disagree, although they are largely and remarkably identical. We rely primarily on two groups of tablets: an Akkadian opus that is usually the principal reference; and the so-called Old Babylonian Tablets. Supplemental material includes a Hittite fragment and the Sumerian fragments.

The Akkadian opus is the most intact; these are principally those twelve tablets found in the temple library and the library of Assurbanipal in Nineveh, and are dated to 7th century BC, and seem "contemporaneous". However, the reconstruction of these tablets, which are badly damaged and unreadable in many places, draw judiciously from other Akkadian tablets, taken from other sites and other centuries. Some of the sources used by Dalley, for example, are actually schoolboy copybooks. The *Epic of Gilgamesh*, as it is rendered, was not created originally as a singular work of literature by the Sumerians who first authored these legends. It existed perhaps as a cycle of tales. More than likely, the written form was preceded by an oral tradition, as was the *Iliad, Odyssey, Beowulf,* and many other long tales and poems of unlettered peoples. The techniques of oral literature are now well known: catch-lines and cliché epithets, repetition in whole phrases and passages, a fluid exchange of motifs and episodes, as if they existed for a grab-bag to the singer or story teller. The *Epic of Gilgamesh* reveals all of these.[49]

More than likely the tales of Gilgamesh could and did stand alone. The oldest tablets to contain text of the "epic" are Sumerian, from several sites and several centuries. They suggest no unified tale as we now know it. In fact there is much material that is not included in the current epic. One tablet or fragment body tells the story of Gilgamesh's death; it is sometimes included by those rendering the Epic, but it was not in the original Akkadian corpus. Another tablet relates his conquest and then his defeat by Aga, king of the city-state of Kish. Still other tablets tell tales of his father, Lugalbanda.

---

[49] Cf. *Background on Translation* for further discussion of the poetic and rhetorical uses of repetition in Sumerian literature.

Background on Translation of Text

Translation of these tablets presents many problems. There is no convention for punctuation. The various languages of the *Epic* do not contain the tenses that we employ in English. It is often not clear which text is first-person, which is third-person, and to whom the third-person may refer.[50] Everyone who translates these texts, or tries to retell them, must guess at some of these things, using context and understanding of the literature and culture to make sense of it. Most of the text sounds or looks like a series of narrations and so favors a rendering in first person, especially so since it often is preceded with a catch-line like "so-and-so made his voice heard and spoke."

The *Electronic Text Corpus of Sumerian Literature* and the translations of Heidel and Dalley translations are literal and precise. As a rule, they seek to find one English word or phrase for one Sumerian or Akkadian word or phrase. As a rule, they place no interpretation on those words, although translators must make guesses in the many hiatus of text, and each one employs slightly different colors to meanings of the text by their personal tastes and ideas. Heidel, for example, follows the quaint convention of rendering sexually explicit passages in Latin.

Literal translations do not provides narrative bridges or explanatory phrases to help the reader, although many provide generous help in footnotes and appendices. Where lines or words are missing, all must show literal gaps.

---

[50] In Akkadian pronouns are not individual words, but are embedded in verbal conjugation or represented by an unvoiced cuneiform prefix to verbs; where verbs are obscured by damaged text, so too is the person of reference.

These problems make these literal translations authentic sources. But they make it very difficult, if not impossibly difficult, for students to read and understand which is why I decided to provide my own retelling for a class that I was to teach.

Any rendition of the *Epic*, therefore, beginning with literal translations, must judiciously compare their variations, resolve disputes provisionally, and because so much of the text is lost or confused, must try to make the fragmentary complete. Sometimes this is an act of discretion. Sometimes it is an act of imagination. I have tried to stay close to literal translations, but I do conjecture where text is ambiguous. I sometimes add some phrasing or reorder the sentences to make paragraphs more understandable. Where my inventions weigh more than the original text, I warn you.

The original text is not a formal poem. I resisted making the rendition a poem, even were I capable of a strict meter, because that seemed inauthentic. Some render the prose of the *Epic of Gilgamesh* so that it "sounds" like an epic. The most endearing and enduring rendition of this genre, although dated now by scholarship, is that of N. K. Sandars, whose popular rendition has been in publication by Penguin Books since the 1950s. Sandars stylized the text to resemble the stately sententious tone of the King James Bible or a Victorian version of the *Iliad*. She even used popular biblical phrases from the King James Bible. In one sense this is appropriate; there is majesty to these words and their meaning that such a rendering conveys well. But this misleads readers, conveying a cultural semblance and a literary continuity that is not true.

The *Epic* is more strange than familiar, I think, reflecting the distance of history and the remoteness of the society. Their customs and sexual mores, their attitude toward death, their religious beliefs, their conception of consciousness and conception of the world—all of these are strikingly different from our own, the modern or the Christian. They are related perhaps to those of the Greeks and the early Hebrews, but they are different also from theirs. I think it is much better to capture the sense of their beliefs and language in their own terms, to the extent that we can, than it is try to assimilate them to our own.

The Akkadian language, as it appears in these texts, lacks the sentence complexity that characterizes English, with its natural tendency for compounding phrases, participles, and adjectival strings. Instead, the sentences are simple, direct, concrete, bursting with imagery. They are often not sentences at all, but clots of words. This language (and, I am told, the Sumerian language too) is brisk and hard-edged. Its cadence thumps like a drum, more than it floats on the fluid of vowels.

For style, then, the common diction and sound of an American story teller seems more apt—descriptive and earthy. But any authentic rendition also demands that it obey the text wherever it can. So there remain the many repetitious passages, stilted expressions, peculiar phrases and untranslatable words. So too remain some passages that are not clear or understandable, not just because of text that is missing, but because the text that is there makes no sense to us. To my taste, this is all for the best. It preserves the uncertainty and mystery that is contained in the original text.

As these passages are read, note the uses of repetition. Repetition, as poetic and rhetorical device, is common in much of the Epic, especially in two conventions: repeated recitations of entire passages verbatim, such as where Gilgamesh explains his intentions to go to the cedar forests (telling first Enkidu, then the young warriors, then the elders, then his mother, then Shamash, in each instance the identical words); and in repeated catch-phrases such as titular epithets. Both conventions are typical of oral literature, where such repetitions facilitate faithful recollection of formulaic verse. Such repetitions shall also have the effect of a given cadence, the effect of chanting, as toward a trance, evoking certain efficacy or meaning.

In addition to these forms, this text also reveals other poetic and rhetorical devices of repetition:

- *commoratio,* which is to essentially say the thing over and over again with variant phrasing (but the same meaning) for emphasis or explication; or

- *epimone,* the use of the frequent repetition of a specific phrase or question, or dwelling on a point; or

- *diacope,* repetition of identical words or phrases some words apart from each other; or

- *epizeuxis,* where the repetitions are side-by-side; or

- *polce,* where words are parallel constructions with different meanings or reference.

To these add *anaphora* and *epiphora*: the preacher's and politician's favorite device to string successions of ideas on the start of or the end of a certain clause, e.g., Dr. King's famous "I have a dream..." speech. We owe to certain ancient Greek philosophers who noted the affects of these on logic and persuasion to give them names, so that we would not be tricked by them (or so that we could learn to trick others). But, whether these identifications give any serious distinction, note again how the cadence of sounds and the trance of meaning is gained thereby.

Background on Meaning of Text

The tablets found in Nineveh were strewn across the temple floor, scattered out its doors and into the street. Those in the chambers of the Palace were dashed and broken, burnt and scarred. If there had been physical organization to this collection of literature and records, it had been ruined by pillage in the conquest of the city. So it is not by the usual meticulous science of excavation that the Epic might have been reassembled.

Fortunately the tablets bear notations, referred to as colophons, at the head and conclusion of the script that cite the ownership, authorship, titles and often enumeration in series. So it is known that the specific order of these tablets of the Epic, in order of one through twelve, is a deliberate edit of the scribe(s) who prepared them.

This fact, and evident thematic and linguistic characteristics of the text, assures that this compilation of what are otherwise widespread folk tales and ancient lore was intentional, was intellectually conceived to create a literary whole, much as a written novel.

Like a novel, the plot advances conscious themes and develops its characters toward a meaningful conclusion. Gilgamesh is changed as a person over its course, first by his encounter with Enkidu, and then by the death of Enkidu. His wanderings climax the "story" of his life meaningfully. His ultimate visit to Ut-napishtim is a curious and seemingly intentional conglomeration of several legends: travel to Mashu (a magic mountain) and through the mountain to the place at the edge of the world where Siduri lives, crossing the sea of death to speak to the one man who has never died, obtaining from him something he must possess, lest he continue to journey in suffering. And in this sojourn the famous tale of the Flood is imparted, made credible and related to the suffering of Gilgamesh, as a part of the answer he seeks, but also exalting him, the first mortal to have learned it; he shall bring this story back to mankind.

What does Gilgamesh seek? Some interpret his adventure as a quest for immortality. In the context of the Victorian society in which this tale was rediscovered, this interpretation is purely Christian and reactionary.[51] By this interpretation, just as this Epic refreshed the veracity of Biblical truth concerning the Flood and therefore divine Creation, this ache for immortality is a prescient presage of the triumphant Christian conviction in divine Afterlife; it is "foretelling" that truth, just as Old Testament presaged to the New the coming of Christ. But such interpretation as this shall be tender nostalgia (and no less inaccurate); it shall be overcast by the fading Christian hegemony to the modern mind, which as the century closed shall be extinguished, although it lies yet in embers beneath the ashes. For in the words of Arnold's "Dover Beach":

> The Sea of Faith
> Was once, too, at the full, and round earth's shore
> Lay like the folds of a bright girdle furled.
> But now I only hear
> Its melancholy, long, withdrawing roar....

Rather, our objective interpretation should be couched in the text itself, in the context of that text's *own* cultural ideology: what Gilgamesh seeks is not "afterlife" in the Christian sense, but the continuation of his life: he simply does not want to die. And more specifically he yearns to be rejuvenated, just as his father Lugalbanda lived so long, having been restored to his youthful vigor by the Anzud Bird in his own adventure.

---

[51] After George Smith soberly put his clothes back on, he rendered the first translation of the Epic and published it in 1876 as the *Chaldean Account of Genesis*.

In the end, Gilgamesh receives from Ut-napishtim a fetish or a medicine, which he himself calls "An-old-man-grows-into-a-young-man," a plant that should cure him of aging. But poignantly this is lost—the "Beast of the Earth" reclaims it and returns it to is original place, as a thing not intended for humans, or as a thing, which like youth itself, is impossible to keep. This conclusion thus resounds the message of resignation, which is the profound meaning that Gilgamesh must take from his heroic life. "It is finished," he declares and returns to his home and the city Uruk.

All of these motifs and the narrative elements of this Epic stand apart in the larger literary tradition, the mythic lore of Sumer and Assyria. We know from the old Sumerian tablets that these appear independently and very anciently. And it is consistent with the convention of oral traditions that underlie this "epic," to conglomerate motifs and tales in such a manner. What is striking, however, is how beautifully the pieces are brought together. Even the middle of the story—those tablets that tell how he killed Humbaba, how he killed the Bull of Heaven—seem "integrated" in a manner that we think aesthetic or psychological valid. For the tales reveal him and elements of the "story" are interrelated, linked to or alluding to portions of text and tale in a linear fashion. The courage of Gilgamesh who would defy death for fame, for example, is contrasted to the fear and despair that consumes him when he confronts the loss of one whom he loved. His coy rebuff of Ishtar's sexual advances becomes the pretext for the story of the Bull of Heaven, which in turn becomes the pretext for Enkidu's death.

These are all acts of mindful intention, it may seem to us, as if there were a single author. The lessons or meaning of the Epic of Gilgamesh, given that it holds the integrity of a work of literature, is therefore more than simply the anthropological interest it has.

This is not just an artifact, or some desiccated sacred text, uprooted from the sustenance of its meaning. The Epic of Gilgamesh must be interpreted as creative literature—as a book of characters, plot and themes. As such, it is the first in history.

We cannot know with certainty that there was a single author. Some tablets themselves bear colophons stating they had been inscribed by the hand of King Ashurbanipal himself. Some tablets cite an author or editor by the name of Sîn-leqi-unninnī. Because the many tablets of many sources are often word for word identical to others found in other sites, distanced also by hundreds of years, the "authorship" is not a simple attribution. This was sacred and traditional literature. It was changed as little as possible by any who copied or edited it. But the editor of this compilation, whoever put these specific tablets together, selected text, changed words, and gave emphasis toward thematic purpose.

That theme is the meaning of death, or perhaps you might say the meaning of life in the midst of death. It is that theme that explains the strange addendum of the twelfth tablet, that otherwise seems out of place. It is that theme that explains the creative renaming of the Babylonian hero of the Flood, Atrahsis, to Ut-napishtim ("he who lives long"—a transliteration of the original Sumerian name) to focus the intent of the episode (see Tigay). It is that theme which choreographs the action and the personal development of Gilgamesh. [52]

The late Victorian and thence customary interpretation of the Epic makes much of Gilgamesh's "hubris," that Greek concept of

---

[52] The Sumerian name for this hero was Ziusudra (also Zi-ud-sura and Zin-Suddu; Hellenized Xisuthros: "found long life" or "life of long days"). The tale of Ziusudra is known from a single fragmentary tablet written in Sumerian, datable by its script to the 17th century BC and published in 1914 by Arno Poebel.

overbearing ego or pride, which is the classical "tragic flaw" of Greek epic heroes. In the tradition of the classical (not to say also Christian or medieval) interpretation, this has come to infer a *moral* meaning or symbolic allegory. But I do not see it. I do not see an allegory or a "tragedy". Nor do I see the so-called "dismal" view of life and death that Sandars, Dalley and others say they see in the Epic.

This perception of a "dismal" view is, I think, the bias of our customary Christian and Western viewpoint. Taken for what it is, as it is written, the Epic's own statement of the "Mesopotamian" viewpoint—for what we have in this text is a conglomeration of several ancient cultures—is decidedly naturalistic, frank and pragmatic. Life is hard. Death is final. This is not "dismal" except in contrast to the idea that I am not supposed to die. I am reminded of the common Western bias against the Eastern religious ideas and culture generally, seeing them as "hopeless" and "bleak" because they do not share the conception of a personal survival from death, nor of a universe disposed toward providential meaning to the individual person. Indeed, the life-long lessons to Gilgamesh are quite the opposite. As Siduri instructs him:

> "So, Gilgamesh, fill your stomach.
> Enjoy yourself. Take pleasure every
> day and every night in every way
> you can. Play. Dance. Refresh
> yourself with baths. Wash your hair.
> Put on clean clothes. Take your
> child's hand in yours and take your
> wife on your lap. That is life."

It is a humble and joyful philosophy.

Appendices

These appendices are selected Sumerian texts related to the Gilgamesh legend, reproduced from the online publications of Oxford University, *The Electronic Text Corpus of Sumerian Literature* (hereafter, ETCSL). These texts are continuously updated and revised based on current scholarship. The web has proved a boon to scholarship and for the open distribution for archaic texts; if it were not for this, I doubt that interest in them should have survived the glut of modern data which seems to be cherished for its immediacy but is none the greater for its wisdom.

The choppy and often obscure text exemplifies the difficulties of reading these in the original and the problems of translating them. Note in particular the frequency of obliterated text and the number of guessed or uncertain meaning, represented by the translators with question marks (?).

The texts shall also parenthetically cite variation of the manuscripts or tablets. The frequency of these may be the less remarkable for considering how often the texts are separated by large distances of space and remoteness in time. In other words, a strong consistency in the texts suggest an exacting tradition to them.

Appendix: The Death of Gilgamesh (version from Me-Turan)

The first appendix is the text of tablets relating the "death of Gilgamesh." There are several extant versions, this one being the most complete. It consists of several segments, most of which are almost completely undecipherable. These two segments are the larger portion of the legend and its import.

SEGMENT A

Lines 1- 12

The great wild bull has lain down and is never to rise again. Lord Gilgamesh has lain down and is never to rise again. He who was unique in ...... has lain down and is never to rise again. The hero fitted out with a shoulder-belt has lain down and is never to rise again. He who was unique in strength has lain down and is never to rise again. He who diminished wickedness has lain down and is never to rise again. He who spoke most wisely has lain down and is never to rise again. The plunderer (?) of many countries has lain down and is never to rise again. He who knew how to climb the mountains has lain down and is never to rise again. The lord of Kulaba has lain down and is never to rise again. He has lain down on his death-bed and is never to rise again. He has lain down on a couch of sighs and is never to rise again.

Lines 13 -19

Unable to stand up, unable to sit down, he laments. Unable to eat, unable to drink, he laments. Held fast by the door-bolt of Namtar, he is unable to rise. Like a ...... fish ...... in a cistern, he ...... ill. Like a captured gazelle buck, he ...... couch. Namtar with no hands or feet, who ...... one by

115

night.... *1 line fragmentary.... unknown no. of
lines missing*

SEGMENT F

Lines 1- 22

2 lines fragmentary.... Then the young lord, lord
Gilgamesh, lay down on his death-bed.... *2 lines
fragmentary....* After lord Gilgamesh had arrived
at the assembly, the pre-eminent place of the gods,
they said to lord Gilgamesh concerning him: "As
regards your case: after having traveled all the
roads that there are, having fetched cedar, the
unique tree, from its mountains, having killed
Huwawa in his forest, you set up many stelae for
future days, for days to come. Having founded
many temples of the gods, you reached Zi-ud-sura
in his dwelling place (*1 ms. has instead:* place).
Having brought down to the Land the divine
powers of Sumer, which at that time were
forgotten forever, the orders, and the rituals, he (?)
carried out correctly the rites of hand washing and
mouth washing .... *1 line fragmentary* ".... *3
lines missing*

Lines 23-37

2 lines fragmentary.... Enlil's advice was given to
Enki. Enki answered An and Enlil: "In those days,
in those distant days, in those nights, in those
distant nights, in those years, in those distant years,
after the assembly had made the Flood sweep over
to destroy the seed of mankind, among us I was the
only one who was for life (?), and so he remained
alive (?) -- Zi-ud-sura, although (?) a human being,
remained alive (?). Then you made me swear by
heaven and by earth, and ...... that no human will
be allowed to live forever (?) any more. Now, as

116

we look at Gilgamesh, could not he escape because of his mother?"

Lines 38-41

(Unknown speaks:) "Let Gilgamesh as a ghost, below among the dead, be the governor of the nether world. Let him be pre-eminent among the ghosts, so that he will pass judgments and render verdicts, and what he says will be as weighty as the words of Ninjiczida and Dumuzid."

Lines 42-62

Then the young lord Gilgamesh became depressed because of (?) all mankind. "You should not despair, you should not feel depressed..... *1 line fragmentary*....Mighty youths and ...... a semicircle .... *14 lines missing*

Lines 63-81

(Unknown speaking) "Go ahead to the place where the Anuna gods, the great gods, sit at the funerary offerings, to the place where the *en* priests lie, to where the *lagar* priests lie, to where the *lumah* priests and the *nindijir* priestesses lie, to where the *gudu* priests lie, to where the linen-clad priests lie, to where the *nindijir* priestesses lie, to where the ...... lie, to the place where your father, your grandfather, your mother, your sisters, your ......, to where your precious friend, your companion, your friend Enkidu, your young comrade, and the governors appointed by the king to the Great City are, to the place where the sergeants of the army lie, to where the captains of the troops lie.... *3 lines missing....* From the house of ......, the ...... will come to meet you. Your jewel will come to meet you, your precious one will come to meet you. The elders of your city will come to meet you. You should not despair, you should not feel depressed."

Lines 82-86

(Unknown speaking) "He will now be counted
among the Anuna gods. He will be counted a
companion of the (*1 ms. adds:* great) gods. ...... the
governor of the nether world. He will pass
judgments and render verdicts, and what he says
will be as weighty as the words of Ninjiczida and
Dumuzid."

Lines 87-99

And then the young lord, lord Gilgamesh, woke
up.... his eyes.... a dream.... a dream ....*3 lines
fragmentary*.... "Am I to become again as I were
.... on the lap of my own mother Ninsumun?....
who makes the great mountains tremble (?).
Namtar with no hands or feet takes away...." *1
line fragmentary*

Lines 100-115

Lord Nudimmud made (?) him see a dream: After
lord Gilgamesh had arrived at the assembly, the
pre-eminent place of the gods, they said to lord
Gilgamesh concerning him: "As regards your case:
after having traveled all the roads that there are,
having fetched cedar, the unique tree, from its
mountains, having killed Huwawa in his forest,
you set up many stelae for future days.... Having
founded many temples of the gods.... *1 line
fragmentary*.... Having brought down to the Land
the divine powers of Sumer, which at that time
were forgotten forever, the orders, and the rituals,
he (?) carried out correctly the rites of hand
washing and mouth washing. ...... the settlements
of the countries.".... *2 lines fragmentary*

Lines 116-130

1 line fragmentary.... Gilgamesh.... Enlil's advice was given to Enki. Enki answered An and Enlil: "In those days, in those distant days, in those nights, in those distant nights, in those years, in those distant years, after the assembly had made the Flood sweep over to destroy the seed of mankind ......, among us I was the only one who was for life (?). He remained alive (?); Zi-ud-sura alone, although (?) a human being remained alive (?). Then you made me swear by heaven and by earth, and I swore that no human will be allowed to live forever (?) any more. Now, as we look at Gilgamesh, could not he escape because of his mother?"

Lines 131-134:

(Unknown speaks:) "Let Gilgamesh as a ghost, below among the dead, be the governor of the nether world. Let him be pre-eminent among the ghosts, so that he will pass judgments and render verdicts, and what he says will be as weighty as the words of Ninjiczida and Dumuzid."

Lines 135-142

Then the young lord, lord Gilgamesh, became depressed because of (?) all mankind. "You should not despair, you should not feel depressed.... *1 line fragmentary....* Mighty youths and ...... a semicircle .... Without him (*i.e. Gilgamesh*)....... Sisig (*a god of dreams*), the son of Utu, will provide light for him in the place of darkness."

Lines 143-153:

(Unknown speaks:) "You must have been told (?) that this is what your being (?) a human involves. You must have been told (?) that this is what the cutting of your umbilical cord involved. The darkest day of humans awaits you now. The solitary place of humans awaits you now. The unstoppable flood-wave awaits you now. The unequal struggle awaits you now. The unavoidable battle awaits you now. The evil (?) from which there is no escape awaits you now. But you should not go to the underworld with heart knotted in anger. May it be ...... before Utu. Let it be unraveled like palm-fibre and peeled (?) like garlic."

Lines 154-167:

(Unknown speaks:) "Go ahead to the place where the Anuna gods, the great gods, sit at the funerary offerings, to the place where the *en* priests lie, to where the *lagar* priests lie, to where the *lumah* priests and the *nindijir* priestesses lie, to where the *gudu* priests lie, to where the linen-clad priests lie, to where the *nindijir* priestesses lie, to where the.... lie.... to the place where your father, your grandfather, your mother, your sisters, your.... to where your precious friend, your companion, your friend Enkidu, your young comrade, and the governors appointed by the king to the Great City are, to the place where the sergeants of the army lie, to where the captains of the troops lie.... the Great City Arali.... *1 line fragmentary....*

Lines 168-172:

(Unknown speaks:) "From the house of the sisters, the sisters will come to meet you. From the house of.... will come to meet you. Your jewel will come to meet you. Your precious one will come to met you. The elders of your city will come to meet you. You should not despair, you should not feel depressed."

120

Lines 173-174:

(Unknown speaks:) He ...... the Anuna gods. He will be counted a companion of the great gods....
unknown number of lines missing

Appendix: Gilgamesh and Aga

The second selected text, the tale of *Gilgamesh and Aga*, is a traditional narrative that relates a political event in the lives of two rulers—Gilgamesh of Urug (sic. Uruk) and Aga of Kic (sic. Kish). As such it appears to be an historical text of an early Sumerian ruler, a tale in Sumerian history *before* the imperialist era of such "King of Kings" as the warlike Sargon of Akkad, when great empires were compiled by ambitious territorial conquests and the wholesale expropriations of rival city-states.

Peoples of the Sumerian plains dwelled in individual city-states, sharing a common culture but politically independent. Territorial issues, especially pertaining to the management of irrigation, evidently concerned them where their interests sometimes conflicted. In this text we learn that two city-states disputing competing irrigation are unable to resolve the issues diplomatically. Gilgamesh seeks authority to use force against the interests of the rival city ruled by Aga. As in the tale of Humbaba in the epic, the elders of Uruk are wary about it whereas the young men are eager for the contest.

Gilgamesh masses the young men and prepares defenses for the anticipated attack by Aga upon Uruk. A siege begins. Aga assaults the gate and enters the city. A defense led by Birhur-tura, repels Aga but he is beaten. Aga implores him to identify his leader, the one named Gilgamesh, but he is not to be seen. Enkidu, who is described here as Gilgamesh's "servant" (and in Aga's words as his "slave") then steps into the breach and confronts Aga who now spies Gilgamesh himself standing on top of the walls and sees how mighty a man he is. Aga is shortly defeated.

The text records the triumph: "Gilgamec cast down multitudes, he raised up multitudes, multitudes were smeared with dust, all the

122

nations were overwhelmed, the land's canal-mouths were filled with silt, the barges' prows were broken, and he took Aga, the ruler of Kic, captive in the midst of his army."

The narrative of military triumph intimates how demanding administration was to the complexity of this economy, how essential good administration was to its success. Canals needed maintenance, barges repair, and armies must be ready. These societies were large and required effective attentive organization.

The conclusion of the text is perplexing. When Aga is captured, why does Gilgamesh address him as his "governor", his "commander"? We should conclude that Uruk had been a vassal state to Kic. Having defeated Aga, the issue in dispute between them was evidently resolved in his favor and/or Uruk had reclaimed its independence. At any rate, Gilgamesh gives leave to Aga to return to his rule in Kic.

If reading this text or the Epic between the lines, noting the assumptions taken for granted by the authors, certain cultural and social characteristics might be deduced. Here, for example, as in the Epic, the "king" addresses an assembly of evidently male citizens to resolve an issue of political will; this deliberative body is a division of elders on the one hand and young warriors on the other. This bicameral organization may reflect the necessity of the martial issue in question, rather than a formal institutional composition. But elsewhere in the Epic we see some such deliberative body also take up other matters of internal and external relations. The "king" is yet autocratic in nature or tradition, and is expressly honored as an "exuberant" warrior. This king is a strongman in more than one meaning of the word. When in the Epic the people seek a champion who is stronger than him, they seek one to overthrow him physically in contest, in the manner of electing a leader as is achieved by a much older folkway of much smaller society than this huge city.

In the Epic the role of the temple in society is also presumed. The specific focus from the outset is upon Inanna (or "Ishtar" in the Akkadian Epic) who is the goddess of that district of the Uruk called Eanna wherein is her temple. The roles of the harlot Shamhat and Gilgamesh's mother Ninsun in relation to this temple; the challenge to him by Enkidu who has been created at Inanna's behest to challenge him and fated to be his "brother;" and in general the continuous tensions between Gilgamesh and Inanna as the Epic's central motif: all reflect a subtext of tension between Gilgamesh and that temple authority and its wealthy district that was dominant in Uruk in his day.

In this tale Gilgamesh is expressly called the "lord of Kulaba," which is an older central district, nearby that of Eanna, one that predates it, even to Neolithic times—that portion of the city in which habitation goes as far back as 6000 B.C. This district is associated with the sky god An, and Anu, his temple complex. The inference may be that just as each district was known to be organized in part, taxed in part, managed in part within its own religious district where its priesthood did enjoy certain special authorities; there may be associated to each district a political subsystem to which Gilgamesh was a part, and his portion of rule was therefore outside of or contingent to the greater district of Eanna and the goddess Inanna.

Lines 1-8:

Envoys of Aga, the son of En-me-barage-si, came
from Kic to Gilgamec in Unug. Gilgamec
presented the issue before the elders of his city,
carefully choosing his words: "There are wells to
be finished, many wells of the Land yet to be

finished; there are shallow wells of the Land yet to be finished, there are wells to deepen and hoisting gear to be completed. We should not submit to the house of Kic! Should we not smite it with weapons? (2 mss. have instead: Let us smite it with weapons!)"

Lines 9-14:

In the convened assembly, his city's elders answered Gilgamec: "There are indeed wells to be finished, many wells of the Land yet to be finished; there are shallow wells of the Land yet to be finished, there are wells to deepen and hoisting gear to be completed. So we should submit to the house of Kic. We should not smite it with weapons! (1 ms. has instead: So should we not submit to the house of Kic? Should we smite it with weapons?)"

Lines 15-23

Gilgamec, the lord of Kulaba, placing his trust in Inana, did not take seriously the advice of his city's elders. Gilgamec (1 ms. adds: , the lord of Kulaba,) presented the issue again, this time before the able-bodied men of his city, carefully choosing his words: "There are wells to be finished, many wells of the Land yet to be finished; there are shallow wells of the Land yet to be finished, there are wells to deepen and hoisting gear to be completed. Never before have you submitted to the house of Kic. Should you not smite it with weapons? (1 ms. has instead: We should not submit to the house of Kic. We should smite it with weapons!)"

Lines 24-29:

In the convened assembly, his city's able-bodied men answered Gilgamec: "'Standing on duty and sitting in attendance, escorting the king's son, and forever grasping the donkey's reins -- who has that much breath?', as the saying goes. You old men should not submit to the house of Kic! Should we young men not smite it with weapons?"

Lines 30-39:

"The great gods created the structure of Unug, the handiwork of the gods, and of E-ana, the house lowered down from heaven. You watch over the great rampart, the rampart which An founded (1 ms. has instead: its great rampart, a cloudbank resting on the earth), the majestic residence which An established. You are its king and warrior, an exuberant person, a prince beloved of An. When Aga comes, what terror he will experience! That army is small, and scattered at the rear. Its men will be incapable of confronting us."

Lines 40-47:

Then Gilgamec, the lord of Kulaba, rejoiced at the advice of his city's able-bodied men and his spirit brightened. He addressed his servant Enkidu: "On this account let the weaponry and arms of battle be made ready. Let the battle mace return to your side. May they create a great terror and radiance. When he comes, my great fearsomeness will overwhelm him. His reasoning will become confused and his judgment disarrayed."

Lines 48-54:

Not five, not ten days had passed when Aga, the son of En-me-barage-si, laid siege to Unug with his men. Unug's reasoning became confused. Gilgamec, the lord of Kulaba, addressed its warriors: "My warriors shall have the choice. (2 mss. have instead: My warriors, choose!) Let someone with courage volunteer "I shall go to Aga" (1 ms. has instead: , and I will send him to Aga)."

Lines 55-58:

Birhur-tura, his royal guard, spoke in admiration to his king: "(2 mss. add: My king,) I shall go (1 ms. has instead: go prancing (?)) to Aga so that his reasoning will become confused and his judgment disarrayed."

Lines 59-69:

Birhur-tura went out through the city gate. As soon as Birhur-tura went out through the city gate, they captured him at the gate's entrance, and then beat Birhur-tura's entire length. He came into the presence of Aga and then spoke to Aga. Before he had finished speaking, an officer of Unug climbed up on the rampart and leaned out over the rampart. Aga saw him and then spoke to Birhur-tura: "Slave, is that man your king?"

Lines 70-81:

"That man is not my king! Were that man my king, were that his angry brow, were those his bison eyes, were that his lapis lazuli beard, were those his elegant fingers, would he not cast down multitudes, would he not raise up multitudes, would multitudes not be smeared with dust, would not all the nations be overwhelmed, would not the land's canal-mouths be filled with silt, would not the barges' prows be broken, and would he not take Aga, the king of Kic, captive in the midst of his army?"

Lines 82-89:

They hit him, they struck him. They beat Birhur-tura's entire length. Gilgamec climbed up on the rampart after the officer of Unug. His radiance overwhelmed Kulaba's young and old. He armed Unug's able-bodied men with battle maces and stationed them on the causeway at the city gate's door. Only Enkidu went out through the city gate.

Gilgamec leaned out over the rampart. Looking up, Aga saw him: "Slave, is that man your king?"

Lines 92-99:

"That man is indeed my king." It was just as he had said: Gilgamec cast down multitudes, he raised up multitudes, multitudes were smeared with dust, all the nations were overwhelmed, the land's canal-mouths were filled with silt, the barges' prows were broken, and he took Aga, the king of Kic, captive in the midst of his army. (1 ms. adds 1 line: Unug's able-bodied men ...... that army.)

Lines 100-106:

Gilgamec, the lord of Kulaba, spoke to (1 ms. has instead: approached close to) Aga: "Aga my overseer, Aga my lieutenant, (1 ms. adds 1 line: Aga my governor, Aga my commander,) Aga my military commander! Aga gave me breath, Aga gave me life: Aga took a fugitive into his embrace, Aga provided the fleeing bird with grain."

Lines 107-113:

(The able-bodied men acclaim Gilgamec:) "You watch over Unug, the handiwork of the gods, the great rampart, the rampart which An founded, the majestic residence which An established. You are its king and warrior, an exuberant person, a prince beloved of An."

(Gilgamec addresses Aga:) "Before Utu, your former kindness is hereby repaid to you." (the other ms. has instead: "I watch over Unug, the handiwork of the gods, its great rampart, a cloudbank resting on the earth, its majestic residence which An established. The city will repay the kindness shown to me. Before Utu, your former kindness is hereby repaid to you.") He set Aga free to go to Kic.

Lines 114-115:

O Gilgamec, lord of Kulaba, praising you is sweet.

Appendix: Gilgamesh, Enkidu and the Nether World

The third tale in this appendix is partially told in the twelfth tablet of the Epic and has been rendered here as the "Adventure of the Halub Tree". That tablet told the tale somewhat differently and also omitted half of it. This is that missing half, telling how that tree came to be planted and so on.

The half of the tale was once translated by the Samuel Noah Kramer and published in his *Sumerian Mythology* (1944):

> Once upon a time there was a huluppu-tree,
> perhaps a willow; it was planted on the banks
> of the Euphrates; it was nurtured by the waters
> of the Euphrates. But the South Wind tore at it,
> root and crown, while the Euphrates flooded it
> with its waters. Inanna, queen of heaven,
> walking by, took the tree in her hand and
> brought it to Erech, the seat of her main
> sanctuary, and planted it in her holy garden.
> There she tended it most carefully. For when
> the tree grew big, she planned to make of its
> wood a chair for herself and a couch.
>
> Years passed, the tree matured and grew big.
> But Inanna found herself unable to cut down
> the tree. For at its base the snake 'who knows
> no charm' had built its nest. In its crown, the
> Zu-bird -- a mythological creature which at
> times wrought mischief -- had placed its young.
> In the middle Lilith, the maid of desolation,
> had built her house. And so poor Inanna, the
> light-hearted and ever-joyful maid, shed bitter
> tears. And as the dawn broke and her brother,
> the sun-god Utu, arose from his sleeping
> chamber, she repeated to him tearfully all that
> had befallen her huluppu-tree.

Now Gilgamesh, the great Sumerian hero, the forerunner of the Greek Heracles, who lived in Erech, overheard Inanna's weeping complaint and chivalrously came to her rescue. He donned his armor weighing fifty minas -- about fifty pounds -- and with his 'ax of the road,' seven talents and seven minas in weight -- over four hundred pounds -- he slew the snake 'who knows no charm' at the base of the tree. Seeing which, the Zu-Bird fled with his young to the mountain, and Lilith tore down her house and fled to the desolate places, which she was accustomed to haunt. The man of Erech who had accompanied Gilgamesh now cut down the tree and presented it to Inanna for her chair and couch. (33,34)

The verbatim text, provided from the ETCSL, is different in several important respects. In addition to spellings (e.g., *huluppu* vs. *halub*; *Erech* vs. *Unug/Uruk*), first, Kramer's text is abridged. Second, the name of the "maid of desolation," who takes up dwelling in the tree, and whom Kramer pointedly identifies as Lilith, is not identified in the verbatim text. Third, the text is ambiguous (as often it is) with respect to the reference of some persons by its use of pronouns. The woman of this text may sometimes be Inanna, or may not be, although presumptively the Sumerian knew to whom it referred.

Version from Nibru, Urim, and elsewhere

Kramer shall abridge all these poetic lines in prologue to the utilitarian phrase "once upon a time...."

Lines 1-26:

In those days, in those distant days, in those nights, in those remote nights, in those years, in those distant years; in days of yore, when the necessary things had been brought into manifest existence, in days of yore, when the necessary things had been for the first time properly cared for, when bread had been tasted for the first time in the shrines of the Land, when the ovens of the Land had been made to work, when the heavens had been separated from the earth, when the earth had been delimited from the heavens, when the fame of mankind had been established, when An had taken the heavens for himself, when Enlil had taken the earth for himself, when the nether world had been given to Erec-kigala as a gift; when he set sail, when he set sail, when the father set sail for the nether world, when Enki set sail for the nether world -- against the king a storm of small hailstones arose, against Enki a storm of large hailstones arose. The small ones were light hammers, the large ones were like stones from catapults (?). The keel of Enki's little boat was trembling as if it were being butted by turtles, the waves at the bow of the boat rose to devour the king like wolves and the waves at the stern of the boat were attacking Enki like a lion.

Lines 27-35:

At that time, there was a single tree, a single *halub* tree, a single tree, growing on the bank of the pure Euphrates, being watered by the Euphrates. The force of the south wind uprooted it and stripped its branches, and the Euphrates picked it up and carried it away. A woman, respectful of An's words, was walking along; a woman, respectful of Enlil's words, was walking along, and took the tree and brought it into Unug, into Inana's luxuriant garden.

Lines 36-46:

> The woman planted the tree with her feet, but not
> with her hands. The woman watered it using her
> feet but not her hands. She said: "When will this be
> a luxuriant chair on which I can take a seat?" She
> said: "When this will be a luxuriant bed on which I
> can lie down?" Five years, ten years went by, the
> tree grew massive; its bark, however, did not split.
> At its roots, a snake immune to incantations made
> itself a nest. In its branches, the Anzud bird settled
> its young. In its trunk, the phantom maid built
> herself a dwelling, the maid who laughs with a
> joyful heart. But holy Inana cried!

The Anzud or Anzu bird (also called Zu bird), which was
illustrated as a lion-headed eagle like the Greek griffin, was the
winged agent of the sky god Enlil, menacing those who
approached his throne, a symbol of Anu (Sky) and of thunder
storms. Anzu stole the Tablet of Destinies hoping to determine the
fate of all things. In a Sumerian legend, the gods sent Lugalbanda
to retrieve the tablets, killing Anzu.

The unidentified woman who transplanted the *halub* tree to Uruk
may or may not be the same who is subsequently described as "the
phantom maid". The original word here is "lil2-la2-ke4" (in the
ETCSL) or lilitû in Akkadian; it is translated in the Pennsylvania
Sumerian Dictionary as "demon," and else wise conceived a "wind
spirit" and is feminine. The Babylonian usage devolves to the
notorious "Lilith," and thus it obtains the associated malevolent
meanings with her legend, but these might not be necessarily
inferred, as Kramer's translation of it might mislead us to believe.

However, the interpretation of the text is not made easier by this
philology. Who or what is the "phantom maid who laughs with a
joyful heart"?

Lines 47-69:

When dawn was breaking, when the horizon
became bright, when the little birds, at the break of
dawn, began to clamour, when Utu had left his
bedchamber, his sister holy Inana said to the young
warrior Utu: "My brother, in those days when
destiny was determined, when abundance
overflowed in the Land, when An had taken the
heavens for himself, when Enlil had taken the earth
for himself, when the nether world had been given
to Erec-kigala as a gift; when he set sail, when he
set sail, when the father set sail for the nether
world, when Enki set sail for the nether world --
against the lord a storm of small hailstones arose,
against Enki a storm of large hailstones arose. The
small ones were light hammers, the large ones
were like stones from catapults (?). The keel of
Enki's little boat was trembling as if it were being
butted by turtles, the waves at the bow of the boat
rose to devour the lord like wolves and the waves
at the stern of the boat were attacking Enki like a
lion."

Utu is Shamash in the Akkadian—the sun or the sun god. Inanna
is sister to him, sharing a father in Nanna, the moon or moon god.
She repeats the opening lines of the tale, relating how the tree
originated and how it was taken and transplanted. Now Inanna
seems to claim that she is the original, the unidentified woman who
had taken the tree and transplanted it. But note that this is not clear
in other manuscripts.

Lines 70-78

"At that time, there was a single tree, a single
halub tree, a single tree (?), growing on the bank of
the pure Euphrates, being watered by the
Euphrates. The force of the south wind uprooted it
and stripped its branches, and the Euphrates picked

it up and carried it away. I, a woman, respectful of
An's words, was walking along; I, a woman,
respectful of Enlil's words, was walking along, and
took the tree and brought it into Unug, into holy
Inana's luxuriant garden.

Lines 79-90:

"I, the woman, planted the tree with my feet, but
not with my hands. I, Inana (1 ms. has instead: the
woman), watered it using my feet but not my
hands. She said: "When will this be a luxuriant
chair on which I can take a seat?" She said: "When
will this be a luxuriant bed on which I can lie
down?" Five years, ten years had gone by, the tree
had grown massive; its bark, however, did not
split. At its roots, a snake immune to incantations
made itself a nest. In its branches, the Anzud bird
settled its young. In its trunk, the phantom maid
built herself a dwelling, the maid who laughs with
a joyful heart. But holy Inana cried!" Her brother,
the young warrior Utu, however, did not stand by
her in the matter.

When Utu is not interested in her complaint, she takes it to
Gilgamesh. It would seem Inanna is always complaining, and
always taking her complaint to some authority or another—male
warrior, father, brother, or assembly of gods.

Lines 91-113:

When dawn was breaking, when the horizon
became bright, when the little birds, at the break of
dawn, began to clamor, when Utu had left his
bedchamber, his sister holy Inana said to the
warrior Gilgamec: "My brother, in those days
when destiny was determined, when abundance
overflowed in the Land, when An had taken the
heavens for himself, when Enlil had taken the earth

for himself, when the nether world had been given to Erec-kigala as a gift; when he set sail, when he set sail, when the father set sail for the nether world, when Enki set sail for the nether world -- against the lord a storm of small hailstones arose, against Enki a storm of large hailstones arose. The small ones were light hammers, the large ones were like stones from catapults (?). The keel of Enki's little boat was trembling as if it were being butted by turtles, the waves at the bow of the boat rose to devour the lord like wolves and the waves at the stern of the boat were attacking Enki like a lion."

Lines 114-122:

"At that time, there was a single tree, a single halub tree, a single tree (?), growing on the bank of the pure Euphrates, being watered by the Euphrates. The force of the south wind uprooted it and stripped its branches, and the Euphrates picked it up and carried it away. I, a woman, respectful of An's words, was walking along; I, a woman, respectful of Enlil's words, was walking along, and took the tree and brought it into Unug, into Inana's luxuriant garden."

Lines 123-135:

"The woman planted the tree with her feet, but not with her hands. Inana watered it using her feet but not her hands. She said: 'When will this be a luxuriant chair on which I can take a seat?' She said: 'When will this be a luxuriant bed on which I can lie down?' Five years, ten years had gone by, the tree had grown massive; its bark, however, did not split. At its roots, a snake immune to incantations made itself a nest. In its branches, the Anzud bird settled its young. In its trunk, the phantom maid built herself a dwelling, the maid who laughs with a joyful heart. But holy Inana (*l ms. has instead:* I, holy Inana,) cried!" In the matter which his sister had told him about, her brother, the warrior Gilgamec, stood by her.

Gilgamesh takes up her cause, kills the snake that has come to make a nest at the base the tree and which no incantations could chase off. He chops down the tree. The Anzu bird flies off with its brood to the mountains, and the "phantom maid," forced out her home, departs for the wilderness. Inanna makes a chair and a bed for herself out of its branches. Gilgamesh makes an *ellag* and *ekidma* (*pukku* and *mekkû* in the Akkadian) which we have supposed as objects of some sort of field hockey.

Lines 136-150:

He strapped ...... (1 ms. has instead: his ...... belt of 50 minas weight to his waist); 50 minas were to him as 30 shekels. He took his bronze axe used for expeditions, which weighs seven talents and seven minas, in his hand. He killed the snake immune to incantations living at its roots. The Anzud bird living in its branches took up its young and went into the mountains. The phantom maid living in its trunk left (?) her dwelling and sought refuge in the wilderness. As for the tree, he uprooted it and stripped its branches, and the sons of his city, who went with him, cut up its branches and bundled them (*1 ms. has instead:* piled them up). He gave it to his sister holy Inana for her chair. He gave it to her for her bed. As for himself, from its roots, he manufactured his *ellag* and, from its branches, he manufactured his *ekidma*.

The "Adventure of the Halub Tree" as rendered begins now where this text ends and is a variation to the remainder. The premise of that tale from the twelfth Akkadian tablet differs from the narrative of the Sumerian in that Gilgamesh decides to chop down the *halub*

137

tree on his own initiative, to make a gift of a wooden bed and chair for Inanna (Ishatar).

The Sumerian text continues in a similar vein, however, to relate how Gilgamesh loses his *ellag* and *ekidma* down in the underworld (it is obscure how it occurs) and how Enkidu is sent down to recover them; it is told how he meets the spirits of the dead and what things they tell him and how at last he struggles back to the surface and is restored to life.

Appendix: Lugalbanda

Lugalbanda, the ostensible father of Gilgamesh, whose statue stood in his bedroom, which he reverentially anointed with butter, and to which he addressed his private thoughts, appeared in important Sumerian legends that told how he had become King of Uruk and other exploits. These are tales in one sense historical, as he is named in the ancient Sumerian List of Kings. On the other hand, magical portions of narrative and the setting of them should make him a figure of myth, of primordial time, of time even at the creation of the world. Lugalbanda is said to have lived and reigned for 1200 years, and so defies mere mortal aspect.

Two Sumerian epic texts feature Lugalbanda, called by scholars *Lugalbanda I* (or *Lugalbanda in the Mountain Cave*) and *Lugalbanda II* (or *Lugalbanda and the Anzud Bird*). In *Lugalbanda and the Mountain Cave*, Enmerkar who was his predecessor as king of Uruk has mobilized an army for war against Aratta. The cause of war is obscured by mysteries in the text. On the one hand, Arrata is a mythic place wherein Inanna the goddess dwells. On the other hand, Arrata is a rival city, which perhaps had been patron of Inanna and whose patronage had been usurped by Enmerkar and stolen for the city of Uruk. On the one hand, the current war is between this city of Arrata and Uruk. On the other hand, Arrata, as a place, has been overrun perhaps by foreign adversaries, the Martu.

At the outset of these texts, which may be taken in series, Lugalbanda is apparently a captain in this army. Passing through steep mountains, halfway to Aratta, Lugalbanda suddenly faints. Unable to revive him, his fellow troops leave him in a cave with provisions and aromatic incense resin, and proceed on their way.

When Lugalbanda comes to, he has dreams and prays for help, but the last part of the text is fragmentary.

In the tale that follows, *Lugalbanda and the Anzud Bird*, he has recovered and found himself in the mountains, lost and alone. In desperation to escape he discovers the Anzud bird on a peak, to which it had taken refuge, having flown thence after the sacred *halub* tree had been disturbed and his frightened fledglings had fled (See Appendix: Gilgamesh, Enkidu and the Nether World.). Lugalbanda cleverly schemes how he should seek its holy favor, in order to receive from him such blessings as he may bestow. The blessings of Anzud should prove his gifted destiny.

Lines 1-27:

Lugalbanda lies idle in the mountains, in the faraway places; he has ventured into the Zabu mountains. No mother is with him to offer advice, no father is with him to talk to him. No one is with him whom he knows, whom he values, no confidant is there to talk to him. In his heart he speaks to himself: "I shall treat the bird as befits him, I shall treat Anzud as befits him. I shall greet his wife affectionately. I shall seat Anzud's wife and Anzud's child at a banquet. An will fetch Ninguenaka for me from her mountain home -- the expert woman, who redounds to her mother's credit, Ninkasi the expert, who redounds to her mother's credit: her fermenting-vat is of green lapis lazuli, her beer cask is of refined silver and of gold; if she stands by the beer, there is joy, if she sits by the beer, there is gladness; as cupbearer she mixes the beer, never wearying as she walks back and forth, Ninkasi, the keg at her side, on her hips; may she make my beer-serving perfect. When the bird has drunk the beer and is happy, when Anzud has drunk the beer and is happy, he can help me find

the place to which the troops of Unug are going,
Anzud can put me on the track of my brothers."

Ninkasi (also given the appellation "Ninguenaka") is the patron of
barley beer. A matron, like Siduri She is also one of the eight
children created in order to heal one of the eight wounds that Enki
receives. She is the goddess made to "satisfy the desire" and "sate
the heart."

Lines 28-49:

Now the splendid 'eagle'-tree of Enki on the
summit of Inana's mountain of multi-coloured
cornelian stood fast on the earth like a tower, all
shaggy like an aru. With its shade it covered the
highest eminences of the mountains like a cloak,
was spread out over them like a tunic. It roots
rested like *sajkal* snakes in Utu's river of the seven
mouths. Nearby, in the mountains where no
cypresses grow, where no snake slithers, where no
scorpion scurries, in the midst of the mountains the
buru-az bird had put its nest and laid therein its
eggs; nearby the bird Anzud had set its nest and
settled therein its young. It was made with wood
from the juniper and the box trees. The bird had
made the bright twigs into a bower. When at
daybreak the bird stretches himself, when at
sunrise Anzud cries out, at his cry the ground
quakes in the Lulubi mountains. He has a shark's
teeth and an eagle's claws. In terror of him wild
bulls run away into the foothills, stags run away
into their mountains.

Lugalbanda, like Gilgamesh, like the Greek hero Odysseus later, is
noted for his cleverness, as well as courage. He will deceive
Anzud in order to overpower him. He will use tricks and glib
speech to deceive him.

Anzud pursued by Ninnurta (god of lightning
From relief of Ninevah circa 750 BCE

Lines 50-89:

Lugalbanda is wise and he achieves mighty
exploits. In preparation of the sweet celestial cakes
he added carefulness to carefulness. He kneaded
the dough with honey, he added more honey to it.
He set them before the young nestling, before the
Anzud chick, gave the baby salt meat to eat. He fed
it sheep's fat. He popped the cakes into its beak. He
settled the Anzud chick in its nest, painted its eyes
with kohl, dabbed white cedar scent onto its head,
put up a twisted roll of salt meat. He withdrew
from the Anzud's nest, awaited him in the
mountains where no cypresses grow. At that time
the bird was herding together wild bulls of the
mountains, Anzud was herding together wild bulls
of the mountains. He held a live bull in his talons,

he carried a dead bull across his shoulders. He poured forth his bile like ten *gur* of water. The bird flew around once, Anzud flew around once. When the bird called back to his nest, when Anzud called back to his nest, his fledgling did not answer him from its nest. When the bird called a second time to his nest, his fledgling did not answer from its nest. Before, if the bird called back to his nest, his fledgling would answer from its nest; but now when the bird called back to his nest, his fledgling did not answer him from its nest. The bird uttered a cry of grief that reached up to heaven, his wife cried out "Woe!" Her cry reached the *abzu*. The bird with this cry of "Woe!" and his wife with this cry of grief made the Anuna, gods of the mountains, actually crawl into crevices like ants. The bird says to his wife, Anzud says to his wife, "Foreboding weighs upon my nest, as over the great cattle-pen of Nanna. Terror lies upon it, as when wild bulls start butting each other. Who has taken my child from its nest? Who has taken the Anzud from its nest?"

Lines 90-110:

Butt it seemed to the bird, when it approached its nest, it seemed to Anzud, when it approached its nest, that it had been made like a god's dwelling-place. It was brilliantly festooned. His chick was settled in its nest, its eyes were painted with kohl, sprigs of white cedar were fixed on its head. A twisted piece of salt meat was hung up high. The bird is exultant, Anzud is exultant: "I am the prince who decides the destiny of rolling rivers. I keep on the straight and narrow path the righteous who follow Enlil's counsel. My father Enlil brought me here. He let me bar the entrance to the mountains as if with a great door. If I fix a fate, who shall alter it? If I but say the word, who shall change it? Whoever has done this to my nest, if you are a god,

I will speak with you, indeed I will befriend you. If
you are a man, I will fix your fate. I shall not let
you have any opponents in the mountains. You
shall be 'Hero-fortified-by-Anzud'."

Lines 111-131:

Lugalbanda, partly from fright, partly from delight,
partly from fright, partly from deep delight, flatters
the bird, flatters Anzud: "Bird with sparkling eyes,
born in this district, Anzud with sparkling eyes,
born in this district, you frolic as you bathe in a
pool. Your grandfather, the prince of all
patrimonies, placed heaven in your hand, set earth
at your feet. Your wingspan extended is like a bird-
net stretched out across the sky! ...... on the ground
your talons are like a trap laid for the wild bulls
and wild cows of the mountains! Your spine is as
straight as a scribe's! Your breast as you fly is like
Nirah parting the waters! As for your back, you are
a verdant palm garden, breathtaking to look upon.
Yesterday I escaped safely to you, since then I
have entrusted myself to your protection. Your
wife shall be my mother" (he said); You shall be
my father" (he said); I shall treat your little ones as
my brothers. Since yesterday I have been waiting
for you in the mountains where no cypresses grow.
Let your wife stand beside you to greet me. I offer
my greeting and leave you to decide my destiny."

So now Anzu shall bless Lugalbanda. But like Christ or Buddha
dismissing the illusions of the world in their moments of trial,
Lugalbanda will have none of what he is offered. First he turns
down great wealth. Then he turns down the prowess of an
invincible warrior. Then he turns down the conquest of cities. He

turns down even the delightful food of the gods, which we may suppose contain supernatural nourishment.[53]

Lines132-141

The bird presents himself before him, rejoices over him, Anzud presents himself before him, rejoices over him. Anzud says to Lugalbanda the pure, "Come now, my Lugalbanda. Go like a boat full of precious metals, like a grain barge, like a boat going to deliver apples, like a boat piled up high with a cargo of cucumbers, casting a shade, like a boat loaded lavishly at the place of harvest, go back to brick-built Kulaba with head held high!" -- Lugalbanda who loves the seed will not accept this.

Lines 142-148:

"Like Cara, Inana's beloved son, shoot forth with your barbed arrows like a sunbeam, shoot forth with reed-arrows like moonlight! May the barbed arrows be a horned viper to those they hit! Like a fish killed with the cleaver, may they be magic-cut! May you bundle them up like logs hewn with the axe!" -- Lugalbanda who loves the seed will not accept this.

Lines 149-154:

---

[53] The Gospels tell of Christ's temptations as he begins his spiritual life, just before he is baptized, in Matthew 4:1-11, Mark 1:12-13, and Luke 4:1-13. The temptations are three: bread to alleviate his hunger on the occasion of his long fast (hence the temptation of the flesh over his spiritual quest); taunting His divinity by urging him to tempt Angels to catch him, should he fling himself from a cliff (hence an appeal to ego or to immortality perhaps); and finally offering him dominion of the world (the temptation of worldly power). The Buddha's temptations occur at the occasion of his Sitting for enlightenment. When on the verge of it, Mara ("illusion") appears to him and offers also food, pleasures, and power. The textual traditions of these details are various. The parallels are a thematic crisis, a thematic temptation, and the hero's thematic resistance and commitment to a defined purpose.

"May Ninurta, Enlil's son, set the helmet Lion of
Battle on your head, may the breastplate (?) that in
the great mountains does not permit retreat be laid
on your breast! May you ...... the battle-net against
the enemy! When you go to the city, ...!" --
Lugalbanda who loves the seed will not accept
this.

Lines 155-159:

"The plenty of Dumuzi's holy butter churn, whose
fat is the fat of all the world, shall be granted (?) to
you. Its milk is the milk of all the world. It shall be
granted (?) to you." -- Lugalbanda who loves the
seed will not accept this. As a *kib* bird, a fresh-
water *kib*, as it flies along a lagoon, he answered
him in words.

Finally, hearing Lugalbanda's refusals, Anzu offers to give him
what he himself would ask for.

Lines 160-166:

The bird listened to him. Anzud said to
Lugalbanda the pure, "Now look, my Lugalbanda,
just think again. It's like this: a wilful plough-ox
should be put back in the track, a balking ass
should be made to take the straight path. Still, I
shall grant you what you put to me. I shall assign
you a destiny according to your wishes."

What Lugalbanda wants is everlasting youth, as Gilgamesh also
would want. This is something other and better than immortality,
for what good is immortality if one ages and becomes sick and
feeble? Better than this is perpetual health and vigor. Perhaps, we
may believe, Lugalbanda did live 1200 years.

Lugalbanda the pure answers him: "Let the power of running be in my thighs, let me never grow tired! Let there be strength in my arms, let me stretch my arms wide, let my arms never become weak! Moving like the sunlight, like Inana, like the seven storms, those of Ickur, let me leap like a flame, blaze like lightning! Let me go wherever I look to, set foot wherever I cast my glance, reach wherever my heart desires and let me loosen my shoes in whatever place my heart has named to me! When Utu lets me reach Kulaba my city, let him who curses me have no joy thereof; let him who wishes to strive with me never say 'Just let him come!' I shall have the woodcarvers fashion statues of you, and you will be breathtaking to look upon. Your name will be made famous thereby in Sumer and will redound to the credit of the temples of the great gods."

So Anzud says to Lugalbanda the pure: "The power of running be in your thighs! Never grow tired! Strength be in your arms! Stretch your arms wide, may your arms never become weak! Moving like the sun, like Inana, like the seven storms of Ickur, leap like a flame, blaze like lightning! Go wherever you look to, set foot wherever you cast your glance, reach wherever your heart desires, loosen your shoes in whatever place your heart has named to you! When Utu lets you reach Kulaba your city, he who curses you shall have no joy thereof; he who wishes to strive with you shall never say 'Just let him come!' When you have had the woodcarvers fashion statues of me, I shall be breathtaking to look upon. My name will be made famous thereby in Sumer and will redound to the

credit of the temples of the great gods. May ......
shake for you ...... like a sandal. ...... Euphrates ......
you feet ...."

After granting this blessing the Azud bird accompanies
Lugalbanda back to his troops who, amazed that he had survived,
gather around him and pester him with questions.

Lines 203-219:

He took in his hand such of his provisions as he
had not eaten, and his weapons one by one. Anzud
flew on high, Lugalbanda walked on the ground.
The bird, looking from above, spies the troops.
Lugalbanda, looking from below, spies the dust
that the troops have stirred up. The bird says to
Lugalbanda, "Come now, my Lugalbanda. I shall
give you some advice: may my advice be heeded. I
shall say words to you: bear them in mind. What I
have told you, the fate I have fixed for you, do not
tell it to your comrades, do not explain it to your
brothers. Fair fortune may conceal foul: it is indeed
so. Leave me to my nest: you keep to your troops."
The bird hurried to its nest. Lugalbanda set out for
the place where his brothers were.

Lines 220-237:

Like a pelican emerging from the sacred reed-bed,
like *lahama* deities going up from the *abzu* , like
one who is stepping from heaven to earth,
Lugalbanda stepped into the midst of his brothers'
picked troops. His brothers chattered away, the
troops chattered away. His brothers, his friends
weary him with questions: "Come now, my
Lugalbanda, here you are again! The troops had
abandoned you as one killed in battle. Certainly,
you were not eating the good fat of the herd!
Certainly, you were not eating the sheepfold's fresh
cheese. How is it that you have come back from

the great mountains, where no one goes alone, whence no one returns to mankind?" Again his brothers, his friends weary him with questions: "The banks of the mountain rivers, mothers of plenty, are widely separated. How did you cross their waters? -- as if you were drinking them?"

Lines 238-250:

Lugalbanda the pure replies to them, "The banks of the mountain rivers, mothers of plenty, are widely separated. With my legs I stepped over them, I drank them like water from a waterskin; and then I snarled like a wolf, I grazed the water-meadows, I pecked at the ground like a wild pigeon, I ate the mountain acorns." Lugalbanda's brothers and friends consider the words that he has said to them. Exactly as if they were small birds flocking together all day long they embrace him and kiss him. As if he were a *gamgam* chick sitting in its nest, they feed him and give him drink. They drive away sickness from Lugalbanda the pure.

After relating his tale—but importantly not explaining his encounter with Azud bird nor the portentous blessing he had received—Lugalbanda takes his troops to place of the battle, a siege previously joined at the dominion of Aratta.

The legend of Aratta is unclear, whether is it land or city, and whether mythic or real; it is unidentified archaeologically. It was formerly the sacred land or physical sanctuary of Inanna until she is wooed to Uruk or those who would be her protectors are defeated.

Here follows then the second half of the tale, which is the tale of how Lugalbanda takes Uruk for his own.

Then the men of Unug followed them as one man;
they wound their way through the hills like a snake
over a grain-pile. When the city was only a double-
hour distant, the armies of Unug and Kulaba
encamped by the posts and ditches that surrounded
Aratta. From the city it rained down javelins as if
from the clouds, sling-stones numerous as the
raindrops falling in a whole year whizzed down
loudly from Aratta's walls. The days passed, the
months became long, the year turned full circle. A
yellow harvest grew beneath the sky. They looked
askance at the fields. Unease came over them.
Sling-stones numerous as the raindrops falling in a
whole year landed on the road. They were hemmed
in by the barrier of mountain thorn-bushes
thronged with dragons. No one knew how to go
back to the city, no was rushing to go back to
Kulaba.

The king of Uruk (and Kulaba) at this time was Enmerkar, which
the Sumerian King's List tells reigned before Lugalbanda. By the
logic of the text Lugalbanda, it appears, was then a mere captain of
the army, leading a small portion of the assembled troops.

From the text that follows it may be understood that Enmerkar had
led his soldiers and others in an alliance of Sumer to combat a
foreign invader, called the Martu, a war-like people who knew no
agriculture and who had overrun the city of Arrata. Enmerkar and
the Sumerians had been failed in their siege for a long time; they
remained frustrated for an entire year. Enmerkar began to worry
over his own city of Uruk, perhaps fearing that might lose the
favor of his people. He needs someone to return to Uruk on his
behalf and seeks a volunteer among his assembled armies.

In the text Enmerkar calls for someone to go to Kulaba. Kulaba is a district inside of Uruk; it is the oldest district in Uruk, dating to a settlement more than 3000 years before the arrival of the Sumerians themselves, and one of the oldest settlements in human history. It is still the heart of power and prestige in the city of Uruk. He wants someone to go as his envoy and assure them that he will win this war. He also wants to supplicate to Inanna, the goddess of the city, on his behalf. For he fears that he has lost her favor. He complains at length about how much he has done for the city, how much he has done in her honor, and yet she seems to have abandoned him in his moment of trial and need

In their midst Enmerkar son of Utu was afraid, was troubled, was disturbed by this upset. He sought someone whom he could send back to the city, he sought someone whom he could send back to Kulaba. No one said to him "I will go to the city." No one said to him "I will go to Kulaba." He went out to the foreign host. No one said to him "I will go to the city." No one said to him "I will go to Kulaba". He stood before the élite troops. No one said to him "I will go to the city". No one said to him "I will go to Kulaba." A second time he went out to the foreign host. No one said to him "I will go to the city." No one said to him "I will go to Kulaba." He stepped out before the élite troops.

Lines 284-289:

Lugalbanda alone arose from the people and said to him, "My king, I will go to the city, but no one shall go with me. I will go alone to Kulaba. No one shall go with me."

"If you go to the city, no one shall go with you. You shall go alone to Kulaba, no one shall go with you." He [Enmerkar] swore by heaven and by earth: "Swear that you will not let go from your hands the great emblems of Kulaba."

Lines 290-321:

After he had stood before the summoned assembly, within the palace that rests on earth like a great mountain Enmerkar the son of Utu berated Inana: "Once upon a time my princely sister Inana the pure summoned me in her holy heart from the bright mountains, had me enter brick-built Kulaba. Where there was a marsh then in Unug, it was full of water. Where there was any dry land, Euphrates poplars grew there. Where there were reed-thickets, old reeds and young reeds grew there. Divine Enki who is king in Eridu tore up for me the old reeds, drained off the water completely. For fifty years I built, for fifty years I gave judgments. Then the Martu peoples, who know no agriculture, arose in all Sumer and Akkad. But the wall of Unug extended out across the desert like a bird net. Yet now, here in this place, my attractiveness to her has dwindled. My troops are bound to me as a cow is bound to its calf; but like a son who, hating his mother, leaves his city, my princely sister Inana the pure has run away from me back to brick-built Kulaba. If she loves her city and hates me, why does she bind the city to me? If she hates the city and yet loves me, why does she bind me to the city? If the mistress removes herself from me to her holy chamber, and abandons me like an Anzud chick, then may she at least bring me home to brick-built Kulaba: on that day my spear shall be laid aside. On that day she may shatter my shield. Speak thus to my princely sister, Inana the pure."

Lines 322-344:

Thereupon Lugalbanda the pure came forth from the palace. Although his brothers and his comrades barked at him as at a foreign dog trying to join a

152

pack of dogs, he stepped proudly forward like a foreign wild ass trying to join a herd of wild asses: "Send someone else to Unug for the lord." [they shouted].

"For Enmerkar son of Utu I shall go alone to Kulaba. No one shall go with me" How he spoke to them!

[They replied:]"Why will you go alone and keep company with no one on the journey? If our beneficent spirit does not stand by you there, if our good protective deity does not go with you there, you will never again stand with us where we stand, you will never again dwell with us where we dwell, you will never again set your feet on the ground where our feet are. You will not come back from the great mountains, where no one goes alone, whence no one returns to mankind!"

"Time is passing, I know. None of you is going with me over the great earth." [Lugalbanda replied]

While the hearts of his brothers beat loudly, while the hearts of his comrades sank, Lugalbanda took in his hand such of his provisions as he had not eaten, and each of his weapons one by one. From the foot of the mountains, through the high mountains, into the flat land, from the edge of Ancan to the top of Ancan, he crossed five, six, seven mountains.

Thus Lugalbanda goes alone to Uruk (and Kulaba) to confront Inanna.

Lines 345-356:
By midnight, but before they had brought the offering-table to Inana the pure, he set foot joyfully in brick-built Kulaba. His lady, Inana the pure, sat there on her cushion. He bowed and prostrated himself on the ground. With (*1 ms. adds* joyful) eyes Inana looked at Lugalbanda the pure as she

would look at the shepherd Ama-ucumgal-ana. In a
(*1 ms. adds* joyful) voice, Inana spoke to
Lugalbanda the pure as she would speak to her son
Lord Cara: "Come now, my Lugalbanda, why do
you bring news from the city? How have you come
here alone from Aratta?"

And accordingly Lugalbanda address Enmerkar's pleas to
her.

Lines 357-387:

Lugalbanda the pure answered her: "What
Enmerkar son of Utu quoth and what he says, what
your brother quoth and what he says, is: 'Once
upon a time my princely sister Inana the pure
summoned me in her holy heart from the
mountains, had me enter brick-built Kulaba. Where
there was a marsh then in Unug, it was full of
water. Where there was any dry land, Euphrates
poplars grew there. Where there were reed-
thickets, old reeds and young reeds grew there.
Divine Enki who is king in Eridu tore up for me
the old reeds, drained off the water completely. For
fifty years I built, for fifty years I gave judgments.
Then the Martu peoples, who know no agriculture,
arose in all Sumer and Akkad. But the wall of
Unug extended out across the desert like a bird net.
Yet now, here in this place, my attractiveness to
her has dwindled. My troops are bound to me as a
cow is bound to its calf; but like a son who, hating
his mother, leaves his city, my princely sister Inana
the pure has run away from me back to brick-built
Kulaba. If she loves her city and hates me, why
does she bind the city to me? If she hates the city
and yet loves me, why does she bind me to the
city? If the mistress removes herself from me to
her holy chamber and abandons me like an Anzud
chick, then may she at least bring me home to

brick-built Kulaba: on that day my spear shall be
laid aside. On that day she may shatter my shield.
Speak thus to my princely sister, Inana the pure."

And, as she may typically do, Inanna answers indirectly, putting a
puzzle before Lugalbanda. A certain heroic task, she suggests,
once it is successfully performed will assure them of victory.

Lines 388-398:

Inana the pure uttered this response: "Now, at the
end, on the banks, in the water-meadows, of a clear
river, of a river of clear water, of the river which is
Inana's gleaming waterskin, the *suhurmac* fish eats
the honey-herb; the *kijtur* fish eats the mountain
acorns; and the ...... fish, which is a god of the
suhurmac fish, plays happily there and darts about.
With his scaly tail he touches the old reeds in that
holy place. The tamarisks of the place, as many as
there are, drink water from that pool."

Lines 399-409:

"It stands alone, it stands alone! One tamarisk
stands alone at the side! When Enmerkar son of
Utu has cut that tamarisk and has fashioned it into
a bucket, he must tear up the old reeds in that holy
place roots and all, and collect them in his hands.
When he has chased out from it the ...... fish, which
is a god of the *suhurmac* fish, caught that fish,
cooked it, garnished it and brought it as a sacrifice
to the *a-an-kara* weapon, Inana's battle-strength,
then his troops will have success for him; then he
will have brought to an end that which in the
subterranean waters provides the life-strength of
Aratta."

As is often the case in literature of oral traditions, some details are
unstated because a common knowledge was presumed. Everyone
knew how this story ended. So, the point of this recitation was to

tell how it came to this point, not to fully detail it; every tale shall have its own purpose in telling.

Accordingly, we are not told—and do not otherwise know— how the matter ends. Presumably Aratta is surmounted and Inanna proves faithful to Uruk after all. However, Enmerkar is replaced by Lugalbanda; this also is not explained, but this is the portended blessing of the Anzud bird's.

Lines 410-412:

"If he carries off from the city its worked metal
and smiths, if he carries off its worked stones and
its stonemasons, if he renews the city and settles it,
all the moulds of Aratta will be his."

Line 413:

Now Aratta's battlements are of green lapis lazuli,
its walls and its towering brickwork are bright red,
their brick clay is made of tinstone dug out in the
mountains where the cypress grows.

414-17:

{missing ms. ....}...Praise be to
Lugalbanda the pure.

Appendix: Selected Sumerian Proverbs

The "proverbs" are taken from the ETCSL source material, from the first six of 28 collections. They date among the oldest tablets found. The enumeration provided is a standard academic identification.

Samuel Noah Kramer, in whose *History Begins at Sumer* (1956) these texts were originally identified as "proverbs," associated them with the Biblical tradition and some of his translations were rendered so as to portray them for direct legacy to portions of the Bible, in a King James edition. They certainly do abide to the peoples of the region, among whom are the Semitic peoples who became the Arabs and Jews of the historical era. Moreover, as succinct expressions of daily life they reveal the common experience and sociology of these lives. They reveal, as has been asserted, how the lives of these peoples established certain normative patterns, which have persisted in other known historical cultures, even to the present day.

For purely literary purposes we have grouped them into categories, so that we might highlight some of their important characteristics. In the original collection there did not appear to be an explicit organization although many seem compiled in topical series.

Proverbs of Profound Wisdom

The profound wisdom of a culture will express fundamental attitudes toward life and the nature of world. We have found the Sumerian pragmatic and fatalistic. He understands the world in terms of what he perceives before him. His world is vibrant with supernatural being, but these are also expressions of what appears naturally.

1.1　Who can compete with righteousness? It creates life.

1.4　You should not say to Ninjiczida (sic. Ningishzida): "Let me live!"

Note: Ningishzida is a Mesopotamian deity of the Underworld, originating with the Sumerian culture. In Sumerian the word literally means "lord of the good tree" or "lord who makes the trees grow right." The root word for tree in this instance also is used for penis, however, and so by implication and by application here the deity has an affinity for forces of procreation and generative forces of nature. He is associated or used for a patron of medicine by some who seek to be healed. His gender is sometimes ambiguous in mythological texts where he (she) is sometimes referred to as goddess.

In Sumerian mythology he appears, on the one hand, as one of the guardians of the Underworld and, on the other hand, as one of the two guardians of Anu's (the sky-god's) celestial palace. His peer and partner guardian is Dumuzi who is Innana's lover.

Ningishzida is depicted in both human and monstrous imagery. Sometimes a bearded man in statuary, he is said to be one of the forefathers in the generation of Gilgamesh. More often, he is depicted as a serpent with or without a human head, and is associated with the psychic and mythic elements of that primordial chthonic symbolism. Ningishzida is represented in the earliest known symbol of snakes twining (some say in copulation) around an axial rod. This representation predates the Greek Caduceus of Hermes by more than a thousand years.

1.7　What has been destroyed belongs to a god. No one is able to take it away.

1.10　My things changed things.

3.20   There are bitter tears in human flesh.

3.120   Offerings create life.

> Note: If abstract, this is profound; if concrete, it reinforces the idea that ritualistic libations for the dead or propitiations made for favorable cultivation or healing and so forth shall be efficacious.

3.141   He who keeps fleeing, flees from his own past.

3.176   I am confronting Fate: "Speak in the way of a just man, or speak in the way of a wicked man, it makes no difference."

4.2   What is placed in the fire has a valuable role to play but leaves nothing behind when it's gone.

4.59   To appreciate the earth is for the gods; I am merely covered in dust.

Proverbs of Practical Wisdom

The practical wisdom of a culture—those factual truths of everyday life—may tell about a society's habits and problems. They are also endearingly familiar.

1.12   Something which has never occurred since time immemorial: a young woman did not fart in her husband's embrace.

1.14   Whatever it is that hurts you, don't talk to anyone about it.

1.28   When a purchase is settled it is soon out of mind.

1.35   Don't pick things now; they will bear fruit later.

1.54   Give me my tools and I will launch my boat.

1.77   Beer is a bull. The mouth is its threshold.

1.103   He who eats too much cannot sleep.

1.105   A heart never created hatred; speech created hatred.

1.189   Food is the matter, water is the matter.

2.71   Tell a lie and then tell the truth: it will be considered a lie.

2.72   He who always lies is a messenger from distant places.

2.121   The good thing is to find it; the bad thing is to lose it.

2.123   The good thing is the beer. The bad thing is the journey.

2.159   Through building my house I incurred debt, so I could not afford to cultivate the field I had sowed with seed.

3.13   While you still have light, grind the flour.

3.15   To eat modestly doesn't kill a man, but to covet will murder you. To eat a little is to live splendidly. When you walk about, keep your feet on the ground!

3.22   A hand will stretch out towards an outstretched hand. A hand will open for an opened hand.

3.69   He who insults is insulted. He who sneers is sneered at.

3.82   He moves like a lion against a louse, but when there is a job is to be done, he moves like a mongoose.

3.159   A good word is a friend to numerous men.

3.161   Putting unwashed hands to one's mouth is disgusting.

4.61   Bitterness afflicted the anus; but it entered by way of the mouth.

5.32   No one will give away even a barren cow for nothing.

5.43   He who rents a donkey for a whole year kindles a fire in the moonlight.

Note: A fire during moonlight is a waste of fuel if just for light.

5.67   No-one walks for a second time at the place where a lion has eaten a man.

Curses and Blessings

Curses, blessings and insults are topical concerns to this society and other societies of ancient history where we shall sometimes find depositories of votive offerings—parchment messages, personal objects, tossed into sanctuary sites of gods or goddesses who are beseeched to effectuate their meaning. In latter days you may find exvoto (notes, personal objects, etc) laid upon or pinned to effigies (and corpses) of Saints in Mexican churches which seek or give thanks for health or good fortune.

1.40   Let his bread be foul food; no man should eat it.

1.41   Let his food be bread and ...... eggs, so that it clogs his throat.

1.42   Let his food be ...... bones, so that it sticks in his throat.

1.76   Like a clod thrown into the water, may it be destroyed as it disintegrates.

1.78   He hurled his insult. He laid his curse.

1.80   It is an insult resulting from an insult. It is a curse resulting from a curse. It is the constant renewal of destiny.

1.81   To accept a verdict is possible. To accept a curse is impossible.

1.178   When you are eating, may nothing lack. When you are in need of water, may things not dry up.

3.8   To serve beer with unwashed hands, to spit without trampling upon it, to sneeze without covering it with dust, to kiss with the tongue at midday without providing shade, are abominations to Utu.

3.130   May you find the response to an insult hurled at you in a dispute.

3.162   May a clever farmer live at home with you.

Proverbs of Social Circumstance, Poverty, and Wealth

The value and relative status of various occupations is reflected in many proverbs, some not here included are carders (in the weaving trades), potters, carpenters-builders, itinerant laborers, and scribes. Among those cited below (and elsewhere referenced in these proverbs) are slaves, fishermen, farmers, shepherds, merchants, and "lamentation priests."

The merchant receives some ambivalent attitude, seen for his necessity but also mistrusted. The fisherman and farmer receive a reverent respect. The shepherd (as also the nomad) has a more dubious reputation. The "lamentation priest" will be mocked like Chaucer's friar. The slave is deplored.

To be poor is miserable, and socially stigmatized. But to be wealthy is its own burden

1.15   Wealth is far away, poverty is close at hand.

1.16   He who possesses many things is constantly on guard.

1.18   Possessions are flying birds -- they never find a place to settle.

1.23   To be wealthy and insist (?) on demanding more is abominable.

1.47   Although the chickpea-flour of the home-born slaves ...... is mixed with honey and ghee, there is no end to their lamentations.

1.50   Chickpea-flour is appropriate for every woman in the palace.

1.55   Let the poor man die, let him not live. When he finds bread, he finds no salt. When he finds salt, he finds no bread. When he finds meat, he finds no condiments. When he finds condiments, he finds no meat. {(2 mss. add:) When he finds oil, he finds no jar. When he finds a jar, he finds no oil.}

1.56   When he walks on the streets no one greets him. And when he comes home to his wife, "Bad Name" is what he is called.

1.57   The lives of the poor do not survive their deaths.

1.67   The city's fate cannot be determined; its book-keeper is a merchant.

1.73   The merchant left the city and the market broke up.

1.74   Things may be traded in the city but it is the fisherman who brings in the food supply.

1.97   Those who get excited should not become foremen. A shepherd should not become a farmer.

1.165   Oh merchant, how you use up silver! And how you use up barley!

2.15   The poor man must always look to his next meal.

2.19   The poor man chews whatever he is given.

2.22   When someone is poor ......, they dine on the broth of the human breast.

2.30   The poor man is this lowly: his debts are paid off with what is taken from his mouth.

2.31   A poor man chewing at silver.

2.c8   He who lives from birds and fish cannot sleep.

Note: A trapper or hunter as in the Epic may have lived a difficult life, even if he is not also an outcast.

3.6   "I will go today" is what a herdsman says; "I will go tomorrow" is what a shepherd-boy says. "I will go" is "I will go", and the time passes.

3.10   If you get rid of the shepherd, then his sheep will not return.

3.23   He who has silver is happy; he who has grain feels comfortable; he who has livestock can sleep.

3.79   A runaway slave girl only pretends to sleep.

3.115   All day long my food ration is kept away from me, my heart ......, but even a dog can satisfy its hunger. It's over for me, but should I be happy? My mother would not give me second helpings.

3.140   Some hulled wheat was made to taste like honey. The nomad ate it and didn't recognise what was in it.

4.43   Left-over clothes are the share of the slave-girl's child; they will fall off her and became nothing but chaff.

Proverbs of Bread:

Bread—in the Biblical proverb, the "staff of life"—distinguishes the civilized man from the beast. In the Epic the beast-man Enkidu does not know what bread is before he is seduced by Shambat and it is given to him to eat. After Gilgamesh's sojourn across the waters of death to visit Ut-napishtim, the exhausted hero falls asleep for seven days; each turn of day and night is counted by a freshly baked portion of bread presented beside him each morning and which slowly moulders.

Bread and water are missing in the Underworld where the souls of the dead wander, hungry and thirsty. Libations of water and offerings of bread are made for the souls of dead loved ones so that they may eat and drink in death. Those without ones to offer them these must starve and thirst. The proverbs of bread preserve the psychic and sacred integrity for this most human of inventions. Some proverbs—especially these—are obscure, containing some intimate cultural suggestions that are not clear to us; some empathy for the culture may make a guess at the meaning but it will be chancy.

1.8   "Though I still have bread left over, I will eat your bread!" Will this endear a man to the household of his friend?

Interpretation: Taking bread offered to you is just good manners, but eating someone else's meal when you should be eating your own is bad manners.

1.21   {One shouldn't} {(1 ms. has instead:) I will not} scorn bread which has turned bad.

Interpretation: If all you have to eat is bread that is dried out and even moldy, it's better than no bread at all.

1.31   One does not return borrowed bread.

Interpretation: You can't give back what you've already used up. Or: "If you break it (eat it), then you own it."

1.51 His bread is finished.

Interpretation: What's done is done.

1.52 There is no baked cake in the middle of the dough.

Interpretation: Don't anticipate what has not been finished.

1.53 My heart urged me to bake two loaves out of a half. My hands were unable to take them out of the oven. Bread is the boat, water is the punt-pole.

Interpretation: Have you ever wished to get more meals out of a pot than it really contains? All you really need is bread and water; bread and water and you are good to go.

3.171 Carrying bread to the oven whilst singing is an abomination to Inana.

Interpretation: Meal-making is a serious business. Remember who gave you the food you owe your life to!

Proverbs about Gender, Marriage and Family

The Sumerian proverb concerning gender, marriage and family shall seem mostly familiar in their attitude. Some gender prejudices, which may seem so typical of those among traditional societies, is in keeping with the patriarchy of the society. But generally, marriage and parenthood are honored in them. Infidelity is complained about. Even choice in love seems encouraged. I am reminded of the endearing bitumen sculpture abiding like a family photograph under the collapsed roof and walls of some old Sumerian home, a man and woman seated closely beside one another, his arm around her, both smiling, an affectionate man and wife as it might be supposed.

Devotional statue, circa 2600 BCE

1.82   What has been spoken in secret will be revealed in the women's quarters.

1.91   My girlfriend's heart is a heart made for me.

1.108 Inwardly a ewe, outwardly a ewe, a most fecund spouse: "Let the shepherd perish, but may you not perish."

1.125 My husband heaps up for me, my child measures out for me; let my lover pick the bones from the fish for me.

1.126 A plant as sweet as a husband does not grow in the steppe.

1.146 Marry a wife according to your choice. Have children to your heart's content.

1.147 May Inana make a hot-limbed wife lie with you! May she bestow upon you broad-shouldered sons! May she seek out for you a happy place!

1.148 Girl, your brother cannot choose for you; whom do you choose?

1.149 Girl, your brother is like me. A brother should let you live as would I.

1.151 When I married a malicious husband, when I bore a malicious son, an unhappy heart was assigned to me.

1.153 He who does not support a wife, he who does not support a child, has no cause for celebration.

1.154 A malicious wife living in the house is worse than all diseases.

1.156 A male aroused eats salt. A female aroused is dragged in the mud (?).

1.157 A disorderly son -- his mother should not have given birth to him. His god should not have created him.

1.158 My wife said "Unfaithful!" to me -- shall I go chasing after women's genitals?

1.159 An unfaithful penis matches (?) an unfaithful vagina.

1.160 Marrying is human. Having children is divine.

1.169 Sons-in-law—what have they brought? Fathers-in-law—what have they disposed of?

Note: presumptively, if typical of patriarchic communities, some exchange of value as a wedding price between the father of the bride and the groom in this case may explain the meaning here.

1.185   A chattering girl is silenced by her mother. A chattering boy is not silenced by his mother.

2.124   For his pleasure he got married. On his thinking it over he got divorced.

2.146   One finds no rest (?) in a house in which a wife does not speak, in which the head of the household (?) does not utter joyous words.

3.5   I will feed you even though you are an outcast (?). I will give you drink even though you are an outcast (?). You are still my son, even if your god has turned against you.

3.112   With my mouth I cool the hot soup for you. I pick the bones from the fish for you.

3.128   May Inana pour oil on my heart that aches.

3.145   For him who is rejected by Inana, his dream is to forget.

Proverbs that Resemble Fables or Arguments

Some of the proverbs appear in series on the same subject or with a narrative manner, so that these proximate lines can appear to be more like a fable, or a meaningful string of aphorisms in the manner of an argument.

Readers may be reminded of Aesop's fables. The common animal characters appear—fox, lion, wolf, dog—and they shall seem to have the much the same personalities.

A Widow's Tale:
      ...... the brothers in anger destroyed their father's

estate. Oh my sister, if there were no outdoor shrines, and, oh my mother, if there were no river as well, I would be dying of hunger. Thus my mother and my younger sister act toward me; ...... am I so deficient in judgment that I should offer my cheek to her? You are not one who stays in one place, you are one who is everywhere. Accept your lot and make your mother happy. Run fast and make your god happy. (1.141-1.145)

Interpretation: these obtuse series of lines imply how the burden of women in widowhood may fall bitterly upon reluctant children or female kin for comfort and aid. The last line is rather more like a weary mother's admonition to son who has caused her grief by his indolence or misfortunes.

The Tale of an Unlucky Man:

"In those places which have been destroyed, let more places be destroyed. And in those places which have not been destroyed, let a breach be made there. Let his place become like chopped-up turnips!" -- Their rituals were alienated. Where there were bonds, that place was destroyed. Their place in the universe was eradicated. -- You should not alienate their rituals! Where there are bonds, you should not destroy the place! You should not eradicate their place in the universe. You should not move the oxen from their places! Let me tell you about my fate: it is an insult. Let me explain it to you: it is a disgrace. Were I to tell my neighbour about my fate, he would heap insults upon me. I looked into the water. My destiny was drifting past. I was born on an ill-fated day. My fate is her voice: my mother can change it. An acquaintance has gone up onto the roof to them. The neighbour is on friendly terms with my

mother in her house. I am one whose fate has
not been determined, confronted by a waif. "I
will be the one who knows how to settle the
account; let me take my position in front of
you," she said to me. I am one whose fate has
not been determined, confronted by a sickness
demon. "I am one who knows wealth and
possessions; let me take my position in front of
you," he said to me. Fate is a dog -- well able to
bite. Like dirty rags, it clings, saying: "Who is
my man? Let him know it." Fate is a cloth
stretched out in the desert for a man. Fate is a
raging storm blowing over the Land. {Fate} is a
dog walking always behind a man. (2.1-2.14)

Interpretation: this series of lines reads like the
lamentation of Ecclesiastes. Where here the speaker
complains about fate, you may hear the other
complain about "vanity." It is similar sentiment.

The Fox in His Own Words:

The vixen quenched her thirst but still her
{teats} {(1 ms. has instead:) motherly teats}
were dry of milk. Each fox is even more of a
fox than its mother. If the hearing of the fox is
bad, its foot will be crippled. The fox's tail is
heavy: it carries a harrow. The fox's door-bolt
is a wooden beam. The fox could not build his
own house, so he got a job at his friend's house
as a construction worker. The fox watered (?)
the barley with rush (?) water: "Nature has
changed its mind." A fox trod on the hoof of a
wild bull: "It didn't hurt (?)!" The fox had a
stick: "Whom shall I hit?" He carried a seal:
"What can I challenge?" The fox, having
urinated into the sea, said: "The whole of the sea
is my urine!" He has not yet caught the fox but
he is already making a neck-stock for it. The

fox said to his wife: "Come! Let us crush Unug [Uruk] between our teeth like a leek; let us strap Kulaba on our feet like sandals!" Before they had yet come within a distance of 600 *nindan* from the city, the dogs began to howl from the city. – "*Geme-Tummal*! *Geme-Tummal*! Come with me to your place! Wicked things are howling at us from the city!" How clever the fox is! He hoots (?) like the *culu* bird. (2.59-2.70)

Aphorism about the Donkey:
My donkey was not destined to run quickly; he was destined to bray! A donkey eating its own bedding. A donkey beating its penis against its belly. For a donkey there is no stench. For a donkey there is no washing with soap. A widow donkey distinguishes itself by breaking wind. One does not marry a three-year-old wife, as a donkey does. Two Akkadians lost a donkey. One went after it while the other wasted the day. The one who just sat around -- the fault was his. (2.75-2.82)

Aphorisms about the Ox: Furrows are pleasant to a threshing ox. An ox following round the threshing-floor is not planting seed. Your dancing (?) ...... is like wild cattle grazing. If the ox kicks up dust, it gets flour in its own eyes. While the ox is ploughing, the dog is spoiling the deep furrows. An ox with diarrhea -- its dung is a long trail! A stranger's ox eats grass, while my ox lies hungry. (2.86-2.93)

The Elephant and the Wren:
{The elephant spoke to himself: "There is nothing like me among all the creatures of

Cakkan!" The wren (?) answered him: "But I, in my own small way, was created just as you were!"} {(1 ms. has instead:) The elephant spoke to himself: "Among all the creatures of Cakkan, the one that can defecate like me has yet to be created!" The wren (?) answered him: "But I, in my own small way, can defecate just as much as you!"} (5.1)

The Lion and the She-goat:

The lion had caught a helpless she-goat: "Let me go! I will give you my fellow ewe in return!" "If I am to let you go, tell me your name!" The she-goat answered the lion: "You do not know my name? 'I-am-cleverer-than-you' is my name!" When the lion came to the fold, {he} {(1 ms. has instead:) the lion} cried: "I release you!" She answered him from the other side: "You released me, but were you clever? As for the sheep, none live here!" (5.55)

Satire about the Lamentation Priest:

The lamentation priest is the whole (?) of the boat. The lamentation priest {hurled his son into the water}: "May the city build like me! May the Land live like me!" The lamentation priest wipes his bottom: "One should not remove what belongs to my mistress Inana." When the lamentation priest met a lion in the desert: "Let him come to the town ......, to the gate of Inana, where the ...... dog is beaten with a stick. What is your brother doing in the desert?" It is the food of a lamentation priest: the pieces are big but the weight is small. The slave of the lamentation priest wails constantly in the market-place: "My food ration is big in size but small in weight. Let me tell you about the size of my food ration -- a lance strikes it constantly throughout the city quarter." A lamentation priest whose incantations do not sound sweet is highly regarded among lamentation priests! (2.98-2.106)

Note: The lamentation priest was a specialist among those serving the temples of the Sumerian city-states. During the Third Dynasty of Ur, the city-state of Lagash was said to have employed 62 lamentation priests who were accompanied by 180 vocalists and instrumentalists. In recent studies of the rituals of these temples they are understood to have performed chants, hymns or "lamentations" to specific gods or goddesses to which they were evidently devoted. The rituals were customary and sacred and obtained features of a cult and liturgical purposes. For example, a "lamentation" was ritualistically conducted for solar and lunar eclipses, which evidently had been anticipated for the occasion of them (Linssen). The aphorisms about this functionary may suggest ways in which his society regarded him, evidently with some irony and humor. The mockery of a sanctimonious priest is suggestive of Chaucer's *Canterbury Tales* or Apuleius' *Golden Ass*.

Aphorisms about the Dog:

Slavering dogs waiting for instructions (?) :......: "Where are you going? Come back! Stay!" Unruly (?), scowling dogs belong to the shameless man. A sniffing dog entering all the houses. A dog eating unclean food is a dog which leaves nothing for the next (?) day. A dog eating ...... ate a pig in the market-place; ...... The smith's dog could not overturn the anvil, so it overturned the water-pot. Patting the neck of a treacherous dog -- patting from the back of the neck. A dog which knows no home. The dog thinks it is clever, but to its master ......

A dog descends, a lance descends -- each does damage (?). The dog licks its shriveled penis with its tongue. In the city with no dogs, the fox is boss. (2.107-2.118)

The Dog in his own Words:

A dog said to his master: "If my pleasure is of no importance to you, then my loss should not be either!" The dog gnawing on a bone says to his anus: "This is going to hurt you!" A dog entered a warehouse. The merchant broke his leg with a wooden door-bolt: "Get out of here!" The dog questioned his tail: "Is there something behind me?" "Those things which make you happy!" it was told. "Well then, let me go back again tonight and receive something!" And so, upon his return, his leg was again broken. He dragged his tail and sat in the street. A second time he questioned his tail: "Did the bolt just come out from in front of you, like before?" (5.78, 5.84, 5.102)

The Wolf in His Own Words:

Nine wolves having caught ten sheep, there was one too many and they did not know how to share out the portions. A fox came along and said: "Let me allocate the portions for you! The nine of you take one sheep. I by myself shall take nine -- this shall be my share!" Imagine a wolf is eating. Utu [Sun] looks down on it and says: "When will you praise me?" "When I'm fat!" would be the reply. While the wolf sat stuck in a trap, he said to Utu: "When I come out, let me henceforth eat no more sheep. When I am hungry, the sheep I've taken, whatever you mention -- what will they mean to me? I shall be bound by a righteous oath. -- Now, what can I eat?" The wolf wept before Utu: "The animals frisk around together, but I am all alone." (5.x5-5.x11)

Aphorisms about the Palace:

The palace is an ox; catch it by the tail! The palace is a huge river; its interior is a goring bull. The palace is a forest. The king is a lion. Nungal overwhelms men with a huge battle-net. Oh Utu, accept my prayer. The palace is a slippery place which catches those who do not know it. The palace cannot avoid the waste land. A barge cannot avoid straw. A freeborn man cannot avoid corvée work. A king's daughter cannot avoid the tavern. The palace -- one day a mother giving birth, the next day a lamenting mother. (2.153-2.158)

Note: Corvée work is unpaid labor for the city, king or temple, an obligation of rank and citizenship, in lieu of taxes.

A Slave Girl's Tale:

You don't know how to spread it out. How your tresses hang down! Your hair ...... one cubit ..... Fatty meat is good. Fatty mutton is good. -- What shall {I} {(1 ms. has 'we'} give the slave girl? Let her eat the ham of a pig! You are pouring the fat from the meat, you are pulling out the roasted barley -- when you carry the cooking pot, watch out for your feet! To be sick is acceptable; to be pregnant is painful; but to be pregnant and sick is just too much. She has risen high, but cannot go on. She is low, but cannot rise. (1.188-1.195)

Note: The lineage of these Palace and Slave Girl Parables are less commonly revealed in the canon of ancient Western (i.e., Greek/Roman) literature, but shall evolve to stock motifs for much middle-eastern literature. The wisdoms here expressed are commonplace to sayings of the Prophet Mohammed and to folk tales such as the *Arabian Nights*.

Like Koan or Haiku Poems

Some of the "parables" resemble poetic impressionistic commentary upon life. Often vivifying a concrete image, sometimes transfiguring it with parallel contrasting imagery or with a generality or other observation, in the manner of the puzzling Zen Koan or the art of the Haiku.

3.107   Something offered is not offered. Something finished is not finished. Nothing changes.

3.1   To stand and to sit, to spur on the donkeys, to support (?) the prince: who has the breath for that?

3.7   Wealth is exposed to the winds. The churned milk, although it isn't river mud, is diverted into cracks in the ground.

3.9   A shepherd his penis, a gardener his hair. An unjust heir who does not support a wife, or who does not support a child, has no cause for celebration.

3.106   Where there is no grain, this is a sign of vengeance turned towards a city. Where there are no reeds, it is the worst of all poverty.

Note: If there are no reeds it shall mean that the marshes have dried up. If the marshes have dried up, there shall be no feasible irrigation for the agricultural fields, hence no grain. Reeds also have other utility to these industrious people.

3.111   Although it has never been there, the goat knows the wasteland.

> Note: Goats can always find something to eat.

3.116   The ox standing in the fodder abandoned the calf to enter the pen.

3.119   Flies enter an open mouth.

3.149   The day became cloudy but it did not rain. It rained, but not enough for people to undo their sandals. The Tigris was not surging at its inlet, so water did not fill the arable lands.

3.150   In Eridug (sic. Eridu), built in abundance, the monkey sits with longing eyes in the singer's house.

> Note: Eridu in its cuneiform means "mighty place. It was the name given to the southernmost conglomeration of Sumerian cities, probably the oldest of that civilization, near the mouths of the rivers which flowed into the sea; this network grew close about temples, almost in sight of one another.

3.153   The goat spoke in the manner of a wise old woman but acted in the manner of an unclean woman.

3.157   The time passed, and what did you gain?

3.166   The sun never leaves my heart, which surpasses a garden.

3.179   He said: "Woe!" and the boat sank with him. He said: "Alas!" and the rudder broke.

3.182   He devours things as locusts do a field.

4.7   All day long, oh penis, you ejaculate as if you have blood inside you, and then you hang like a damp reed.

4.56   Says the man lying on the roof to the man living in the house: "It is too bright up here!"

Al-Rawi, Farouk N H and George, Andrew (2014) "Back to the Cedar Forest: The beginning and end of Tablet V of the Standard Babylonian Epic of Gilgameš." *Journal of Cuneiform Studies*, 66 . pp. 69-90.

Black, J.A., Cunningham, G., Fluckiger-Hawker, E, Robson, E., and Zólyomi, G., *The Electronic Text Corpus of Sumerian Literature* (http://www-etcsl.orient.ox.ac.uk/), Oxford 1998-2006. Copyright © J.A. Black, G. Cunningham, E. Robson, and G. Zólyomi 1998, 1999, 2000; J.A. Black, G. Cunningham, E. Flückiger-Hawker, E. Robson, J. Taylor, and G. Zólyomi 2001; J.A. Black, G. Cunningham, J. Ebeling, E. Robson, J. Taylor, and G. Zólyomi 2002, 2003, 2004, 2005; G. Cunningham, J. Ebeling, E. Robson, and G. Zólyomi 2006. The authors have asserted their moral rights.

Dalley Stephanie. *Myths from Mesopotamia: Creation, The Flood, Gilgamesh, and Others*. Oxford University Press: Oxford, 1989.

Damrosch, David. *The Buried Book: The Loss and Rediscovery of the Great Epic of Gilgamesh*. New York: Holt. 2006.

George, A.R. *The Babylonian Gilgamesh Epic*. Vol. 1. Oxford: Oxford. 2003.

Heidel, Alexander. *The Epic of Gilgamesh and Old Testament Parallels*. University of Chicago Press: Chicago, 1963.

Kramer, Samuel Noah. *History Begins at Sumer*. Philadelphia: University of Pennsylvania. 1956.

Linssen, Marc J. H. *Cuneiform Monographs, #25: The Cults of Uruk and Babylon: The Temple Ritual Texts as Evidence for Hellenistic Cult Practice*. Leidin: Brill. 2004.

Tigay, Jeffrey H. *The Evolution of the Gilgamesh Epic*. Philadelphia: University of Pennsylvania Press. 1982.

John Harris began his writing career at age 60, about the same time that he began his teaching career. He lives in Wabasha, Minnesota. His published works currently include:

- *The Epic of Gilgamesh*—an annotated prose rendition of the ancient epic, based upon original Akkadian, Sumerian, Babylonian and Hittite texts with appendices
- *Faustbook*—a narrative poem in five acts retelling the legend of Faust with a contemporary meaning
- *The Lives and Opinions of Eminent Philosophers, Vol. I & Vol. II*—a collection of short stories and novellas which are predicated upon the lives of certain ancient Greek philosophers, upon which original text this title is based
- *Mrs. Wilson's Tales*—a compilation of authentic tales of the Kathlamet, an extinct native American tribe of the Pacific Northwest, and retold versions of the same tales, cast in the epoch of Wisconsin pioneers of the 18th and 19th centuries.
- *Conscience in Extremis: An Essay on Morality in History*— a book-length essay in consideration of the moral conflicts of the American Sixties with particular emphasis upon the lives of Norman Morrison and Robert S. McNamara, one a martyr and the other an architect of the Vietnam War. The wider question of the import of this epoch to our present and future times is drawn by its analysis and conclusion
- *fishes* – collected poetry
- *The Tragical History of Doctor Faustus*—annotated Elizabethan play of Christopher Marlowe with background and supplements.

John is working on Volume III of *Lives and Opinions*, *The Lore of Gawain* (a compendium of medieval literature), a retelling of the *Lais of Marie de France*, and an untitled essay on the state of public education. More of his writings and podcasts of his books in audio are available at www.ieros.info.